BRIAN CLARKE

BRIAN CLARKE
ARCHITECTURAL ARTIST

AD ACADEMY EDITIONS

Art & Design Monographs
Editorial Office: 42 Leinster Gardens London W2 3AN

Art Editor: Andrea Bettella
House Editor: Nicola Hodges
Editorial and Design Team: Mark Lane, John Ashing

Acknowledgements
Photography: Stuart Blackwood, Black & White Communications, Martin Booth,
Barry Ord Clark, Prudence Cuming Associates, Kipper Dodds, Future Systems,
Dieter Leistner, Mo Rana, Shinkenchiku-Sha, Gino Sprio, Yoshio Takase – Retoria, Richard Waite
Stained Glass Fabrication: Derix Glass Studios, Taunusstein
Stained Glass Montages: Maria Jose Beldock
Model Making at Brian Clarke's Studio: Mark Thaler
Architects: Alsop & Störmer, Bieling & Bieling, Bernard Engle, Sir Norman Foster & Partners,
Future Systems, von Gerkan & Marg & Partners, Wilhelm Helms, Naoki Iijima,
Arata Isozaki & Associates, Derek Latham & Company, Cobb, Fried & Partners,
Renton Howard Wood Levin Partnership, Trehearne & Norman
Assistants: Martin Booth, Mark Keegan, Mohammed Rana, Mark Thaler
Also: MPL Communications Ltd

Cover: Haus der Energie, Kassel
Page 2: The Victoria Quarter, Leeds
Page 128: Portrait of Brian Clarke. Photograph by Gino Sprio

First published in Great Britain in 1994 by
ACADEMY EDITIONS
An imprint of the Academy Group Ltd

ACADEMY GROUP LTD
42 Leinster Gardens London W2 3AN
Member of VCH Publishing Group

ISBN 1 85490 343 8 (PB)
ISBN 1 85490 345 4 (HB)

Distributed to the trade in the United States of America by
ST MARTIN'S PRESS
175 Fifth Avenue, New York, NY 10010

Printed and bound in Singapore

CONTENTS

ESSAYS

PAINTINGS

PROJECTS

Eloquence from Intractability

Martin Harrison

As an architectural artist, Brian Clarke has worked in many different media, including mosaic and tapestry, but this essay concentrates primarily on his stained glass. The omission of more than a brief reference to his paintings is unavoidable, though it should be stressed that painting and drawing not only replenishes his stained glass but in fact generates his abstract language of forms. The wandering, nervy, linear passages that distinguished many of his windows up until the early 1980s have their source in the life-drawings that remain a vital discipline in his art, just as the sweeping calligraphy and the organic elements of his more recent windows originate in his paintings. Unlike painting, stained glass is activated by transmitted, as opposed to reflected, light. Indeed, it was the constant changes in the nature and intensity of natural light – its kinetic modulation – which attracted Clarke to work in stained glass. Disinclined to reduce their light transmission, he forsakes the application of opaque paint on his windows, working only with the basic essentials, glass and lead, wrenching bravura performances from these simple and often intractable ingredients.

In terms of both their scale and diversity his stained glass commissions through the world have placed him in a pre-eminent position among living artists working in the medium, and he has collaborated with some of the world's leading architects. But the subject of stained glass continues to present an apparently insuperable obstacle for many art historians and critics. Even scholars of medieval art deplore the fact that had the great windows of, say, Chartres or Canterbury Cathedrals been created in any other medium, the attention paid to them would be infinitely greater. The subject is inadequately researched and the literature is patchy at best, and if this is true for medieval glass, the situation regarding modern stained glass is worse. In a century which has witnessed the multiple deaths of easel art (at the hands, for example, of Duchamp, the Futurists, the Russian Constructivists and the Conceptualists), the resistance to embracing the relevance of an art ineluctably allied to architecture (and distanced, therefore, from commodity capitalism) remains a paradox.

There is no rational basis for the prejudice against stained glass. The narrowness of the fine art camp frequently extends even to ignoring the subject of architecture itself. It is an irony of twentieth-century art criticism that even Marxist theorists have devoted themselves to endless worrying or posturing over autonomous easel art, while ignoring the truly public arts which have the potential to shape our environment directly and radically.

Brian Clarke's position in this debate is interesting, since he is not only an architectural artist but also the maker of easel paintings. His paintings are occasionally destined for a specific architectural interior, but are more often autonomous. He is, in other words, a fine artist who also functions as an architectural artist. What he has attempted to do from the outset of his career is to combine both of these roles, compromising with neither. There are, of course, differences. His stained glass is required to relate to the size and shape of the window opening(s) and to the ambient lighting, in addition to a multitude of internal and external environmental factors. The design must respond to all of these disciplines and manifestly requires the kind of organisation which precludes the spontaneity which may attend the act of painting. To some extent, his painting and stained glass have developed along parallel paths, sustaining one another in a symbiotic relationship. For more than 20 years Clarke has succeeded in a delicate balancing act between the two media.

The position Clarke occupies in the contemporary art world is a difficult one, and his success has not been achieved without controversy. On the one hand, fine art critics are nervous or uncomprehending about an artist who is perceived to be associated with the applied arts. They prefer to assign the dubious epithet of the 'lesser' arts to the architectural media in which he works, reserving for easel art the higher cultural ground (though, as John Piper asserted, 'art is minor only when it is mediocre'). Yet, in no significant sense is Clarke's art undermined when he works in an architectural situation. He has to *adapt* his vocabulary to certain givens, but it is untenable to suggest that this necessarily entails a dilution of his vision. No art before the Renaissance was anything other than 'applied' – a definition which would have to be attached, for instance, both to mural and manuscript painting. If such an association automatically eliminated art-works from serious consideration, not only would all medieval painting have to be written out of art history but also a large proportion of the oeuvres of, say, Van Eyck, Michelangelo, Raphael and even many post-Renaissance artists.

On the other hand, too few architects have absorbed the lessons of the past and have lost either the desire or the ability to collaborate with artists. Also, it must be admitted that the buildings containing Clarke's stained glass are of uneven merit in themselves. This is something over which he has no control, though it is encouraging to note that among those with whom he has closely collaborated are Norman Foster, Will Alsop, Arata Isozaki and Future Systems.

A further problem for many critics is the *craft* element of stained glass. (It might be added that the ecclesiastical links are frequently cited as a disincentive.) Clarke's position regarding this issue requires some explanation. His interest in the medium dates back to his learning, while still at Burnley Art School, of the English Pre-Raphaelite painters, and the discovery that a circle of painters associated with William Morris, including Rossetti, Burne-Jones and Madox Brown, had also designed stained glass windows. In turn, these were made by Morris' firm. Clarke's youthful fascination with the Pre-Raphaelites grew into an intense interest when, in 1970, he enrolled on a two-year course devoted to 'Architectural Stained Glass' at North Devon College of Art. Though the direct inspiration from Pre-Raphaelism was short-lived, the lessons of some of the group's principles were of more enduring significance. The fact that some of England's leading artists of the 1860s had produced designs for stained glass, with no apparent detriment to their painting, was a revelation of the utmost importance for him. It seemed to point the way for his own future, which, as he saw it, might equally encompass working in more than one medium.

In 1970, if Clarke was to design stained glass windows then he would have to learn how to make them, too. There was no alternative – stained glass was taught solely as a craft in colleges throughout Britain at this time. Questions of design or fitness for the architecture were either ignored or considered to be secondary. This was an indication of the persistence of the (imperfectly understood) ideals of the Arts and Crafts movement; Ruskin's dictum of 'truth to materials' was interpreted as meaning that only the involvement with all aspects of the crafts process would result in better design, based on the romantic notion that great designs evolved without external assistance from the hands of medieval craftsmen. In the event, Clarke's craft training did no harm. Since his mature designs necessitated the development of some innovatory techniques and materials, he was more than capable of directing the fabricators of his windows as to the application of these techniques. The selection of appropriate glass colour and texture remains an important aspect of his work, which he undertakes personally and with great care.

William Morris, too, believed that architecture was the mother of the arts and crafts, an idea that became a central tenet of the Arts and Crafts movement; however, in practice, Morris' methods diverged considerably from his theories. In the actual manufacture of his stained glass windows, for instance, neither Rossetti, Burne-Jones nor Madox Brown ever took any active part; their contributions ceased at the design and cartoon stage. All of the subsequent stages in their execution – cutting, painting, firing, leading and fixing – were performed by specialist craftsmen under Morris' supervision. This was not a Ruskinian fusion of art and craft but a strict separation of the two. Yet the windows that sprung from this method of devolved teamwork were widely recognised as among the finest made since the Middle Ages. Clarke believed that, like his Pre-Raphaelite forebears, his art would develop only if he devoted all of his energies to it, rather than the time-consuming craft processes; the artist who ignores this warning is, as again John Piper so wisely warned, in danger of 'trimming his original gift'. Since 1978 all of Clarke's windows have been made outside his studios, albeit under his close supervision.

While the fabrication of a stained glass window involves craftwork, and Clarke directs this insofar as the faithful realisation of his ideas are concerned, the situation is in many ways no different from making a painting. It is simply that the raw materials of Clarke's language are glass and lead, as opposed to paint and canvas.

The first windows Clarke made independently were for churches, and their iconography was partly figurative. They showed some originality, but he realised that in England he was working in a creative vacuum. The award of a Winston Churchill Trust Travelling Fellowship in 1974, provided for him to visit Germany, Paris and Rome, and proved to be a turning point in his career. In effect, these tours enabled him to overcome the limitations of his craft-oriented art college training and facilitated the serious study of sources in twentieth-century architecture, painting and stained glass. Subjects on which his knowledge was steadily expanding.

The Modern movement in architecture had struggled to take hold in Britain in the 1930s, and none of the leading practitioners was British. The situation at that time in stained glass was similar. There were, at most, two or three artists working in modernist styles, while the great majority clung to either the fag-end of Gothic Revivalism or worked-out Arts and Crafts ideals. Around 1900, however, Britain had still been widely considered to be an important force in architecture and associated arts. In Germany, one of the countries which picked up the torch of modernism, Hermann Muthesius' book *Das Englische Haus* (1904), had, ironically, been an important influence on a generation of emergent modernist architects and designers – the muse migrated to the *werkbund*. There also grew up in Muthesius' time a flourishing contemporary school of stained glass in Germany, inspired at first by the example of the expatriate Dutchman Jan Thorn Prikker. An artistic lineage was established which still persisted into the 1970s, with a substantial group of stained glass artists working in identifiably 'modern' styles. A few stained glass windows had been designed by distinguished French artists and architects since 1945 (Léger at Audincourt, Matisse at Vence, Le Corbusier at Ronchamp), but they were isolated examples, and it was in Germany that Clarke decided to research his antecedents and contemporaries.

The search for early twentieth-century precursors in stained glass – at the roots, as it were, of the Modern movement – was important for Clarke. There was no discernible British tradition to which he could align himself, and the existence of evolutionary links elsewhere in Europe helped provide a framework for his own ideas about stained glass, a theoretical basis from which he might develop. The discovery that in 1921 Thorn Prikker had rejected the Symbolist and Expressionist styles of his earlier stained glass, in favour of a geometrical abstraction, was of great significance. Though surviving examples were scarce, Clarke was also able to locate stained glass by other notable pioneers of abstraction, including Sophie Taeuber-Arp, Josef Albers and members of the Dutch De Stijl group. Prototypes like these supplied further evidence that there was a moment, in the immediate past, when leading artists had designed for stained glass.

Even before a stained glass department was founded at the Bauhaus, three De Stijl artists, Theo van Doesburg, Bart van der Leck and Wilmos Huszar, had designed stained glass, and the evidence suggests that it was their experiments with grid-based window designs which provided the push towards the gridded formats of their abstract paintings. A comparison with Clarke's designs is suggested here, but he has always extended beyond the geometry of the grid, or matrix, which is the basis of his compositions, to challenge and disturb the order he has established by introducing a provocative counter-theme.

More immediately relevant though, on his first trip to Germany, was the contact he made with contemporary stained glass designers, and in particular Johannes Schreiter. He was greatly encouraged by the fact that Schreiter was first and foremost an artist. Schreiter stood somewhat outside the mainstream of German art and certainly had little obvious affinity with artists such as Joseph Beuys or Gerhard Richter, with whose work Clarke was familiar. But he had been able to translate his austerely graphic, organic, fragmented style into stained glass with remarkable originality. Moreover, the ascetic Schreiter brought to his stained glass designs a rigorous intellect and uncompromising purity of approach that stood as crucial exemplars for the younger artist.

The experiences of Germany were synthesised by Clarke into a philosophy that was only partly related to what he had learned there. In what was to become a key point of departure in his own work, he came to appreciate that he was, in short, working within the tradition of Constructivism. (That he continued to identify with this movement is underlined by the title of the essay *Toward a New*

All Saints Church, Habergham, Lancashire

Olympus Optical Europa, Hamburg

Constructivism, which was his contribution to the influential book he edited, *Architectural Stained Glass*, published in 1979.) Central to his alignment with this tradition was the belief in the Constructivists' aim of dissolving the barriers between architecture, painting and the applied arts. Although he may have greatly admired the works of the Russians, Malevich, Rodchenko and El Lissitsky, he had no intention of imitating them. He was, however, profoundly affected by a fundamental precept of Constructivism, the dialectic between the static and the dynamic, between order and chaos. It was a duality which remained at the core of his art, and consequently of his stained glass designs. As his understanding of architecture deepened, so did his resolve that the architectural context would provide the starting point for his designs, which would be structural rather than merely decorative. The 'static' or 'ordered' base of his designs (the grid) defines and articulates the architectural space, the 'dynamic' or 'chaotic' elements subtly erode it. The contradiction this seems to imply is apparent rather than real, for the subversive elements of his compositions, which can, of course, only be metaphorically 'destructive', ultimately draw attention to the architecture within which they are contained, accentuating its inherent structure.

It should be clear, then, that Clarke did not adopt Constructivism in its totality. It would in any case have been naive for him to continue to subscribe to a nebulous utopian techno-future. Neither was he an adherent of the 'New-Constructivism' being propounded by Joost Baljeu or Max Bill. But he was inspired by the passion of statements made by Rodchenko at the XIX State Exhibition in Moscow in 1920: 'Non-objective painting has left the museums; non-objective painting is in the street itself, the squares, the towns and the whole world. The art of the future will not be the cosy decoration of family homes. It will be just as indispensable as 48-storey skyscrapers, mighty bridges, wireless, aeronautics and submarines which will be transformed into art.' From this kind of revolutionary dogma he extracted what was meaningful for him and integrated it into his own art, which would be more accurately described as having grown out of Constructivism.

The lessons he learned in Europe confirmed and consolidated the direction which he had been taking in stained glass. In 1975, he was awarded a further grant by the Churchill Trust which enabled him to visit the USA. He was particularly impressed by Mies van der Rohe's drawings, of which he had made a careful study at the Museum of Modern Art, New York, and Mies van der Rohe's Barcelona Pavilion figured in several 'Tributes' he painted on his return. The paintings were, as much as anything, an announcement of the primacy of architecture, but, in the same year, the opportunity to realise his ideas on any significant scale in stained glass was still limited to ecclesiastical commissions. Another important influence was Japanese screen-paintings, with which he had long been familiar but first encountered in volume in an exhibition held at this time at the British Museum. Not only the calligraphic fluency of the screens but also their sequential nature is evident in a series of windows he designed for Longridge church, Lancashire (1975). A major advance on his earlier stained glass, the Longridge series may be considered the first stained glass of Clarke's maturity. Referring in a non-literal way to the surrounding landscape, the 20 abstract 'panels' present a disarmingly sophisticated extension, or revision, of the narrative and didactic traditions of stained glass. They insist on being 'read' in sequence, incorporating the kinetics of fluctuations in the lighting conditions and the amount of time the viewer takes to move from window to window.

Several other commissions for church windows followed, of which one of the most effective (no doubt because the building itself, by FX Velarde, offered Clarke unusual stimulation) was for two tall, thin lancets in the baptistery of the church of St Gabriel, Blackburn. A rare example for England of modernistic ecclesiastical architecture of the 1930s, St Gabriel's interior walls were painted cream, and some of the original chrome fittings survived. Having set up an architectonic, compositional order, it is subtly interrupted when, at just one point, the milky opalescent glass which occupies most of the window capriciously invades the blue and green border. Graphic complexity is reserved for the rounded window heads, and it is hard to imagine anything more appropriate for its setting than this stately, elegant design.

His confident handling of space is further exemplified by the powerful east window at Habergham Eaves church, Lancashire (1976). Comparatively reticent in both colour and design in the lower portions of the five main lights, the upper half, in a stunning and hauntingly dramatic gesture, is thrown out of vertical axis, the dislocated section exploding into rainbow colours, intersecting the gothic tracery. The design of Habergham Eaves church has been variously interpreted as a complex spiritual tract ('representing' creation, judgement, the elements) and as an indicator of Clarke's punk affiliations. As someone with a particular interest in the subject, I should like to hail it as the great dissonant masterpiece of English ecclesiastical stained glass of the twentieth century.

This phase of his career, however, effectively came to an end in 1977 and was marked by his gift of three windows to the church at Birchover in Derbyshire, the village he was shortly to leave for London. The Birchover series wittily plays with a stained glass convention, the medallion, which traditionally contained a figure subject and was usually surrounded by a 'canopy' or foliage patterns. In place of biblical scenes in his 'medallions' Clarke substitutes grids of broken horizontals. It was an idea he was later to exploit even more teasingly in a window for what was formerly the London studio of a nineteenth-century stained glass firm, Lavers & Barraud (1981). Here, he reversed historical precedent by making the ten rectangular 'medallions' the negative passages in the design. Against a deep blue background and set off by ruby borders (a colour scheme which, in ironically quoting one of their conventions, makes humorous reference to the building's Victorian occupants), the only 'incidents' the medallions frame are the pale blue streaks inherent in the texture of their white opalescent glass. As he has often stated, colour and line can be as eloquent as the human figure.

The church authorities found his windows hard to accept, and if he bowed to their conservatism he might well have boxed himself into a cosy corner. As it was, 1977 marked the end of his relationship with the Church of England. Fortunately, in 1977-78 he reached another milestone in his career with a major commission for both stained glass and paintings at the Queen's Medical Centre, University of Nottingham. Large-scale secular commissions began to follow, including another which combined stained glass and paintings for the Olympus Optical Co Headquarters building in Hamburg (1981). His scheme for the Mosque at King Khaled International Airport, Riyadh (1982), was a considerable success on its own terms and also another important formative exercise. He managed to work around the enforced discipline of repetitive Islamic traditional patterns to produce designs which both remained personal and avoided tedium.

The persistence of repetition in both paintings (for example, the cross symbol) and stained glass invites comparison with so-called minimal music. For Clarke, repetition appears to have links with the industrial/machine aesthetic and the infinitely reproducible, but he clearly shares with composers such as La Monte Young and Steve Reich an interest in investigating non-Western cultures, and in inducing rhythmic trance-like, meditative or ecstatic states.

His consummate spatial ability and grasp of scale were now widely recognised, and in 1987 Clarke embarked on the first of a group of projects for literally immense roof spaces, with his design for Buxton Thermal Baths. If designing for stained glass normally entails filling a void in a wall – the transition from substance to space – glazing a roof-space necessitates an alternative approach, since the light to be filtered is from a different direction and there is not the contrast, the abrupt graduation of wall and window. (We tend to assume that stained glass is always intended to occupy a prescribed shape of opening in a wall, but it should be emphasised that Clarke is adept at coping, undaunted, with the problems presented by this sort of architectural *tabula rasa*, the complete wall, or roof, where, in providing the 'frame', he acts almost as an architect himself.) What Clarke achieves in his magisterial design for Buxton is a reconciliation of the twin aims of the subtle modulation of the vagaries of the ambient lighting. And a composition which respects the great curved plane of the roof added to Sir Joseph Paxton's building remains full of incident. Besides the organic splotches of colour which oscillate throughout the window there is a group of motifs which originated in his paintings in the early 1980s and which might be described as a fragmented kind of Greek-key; an appropriately architectural device 'unlocked' with virtuoso diversity. Also at Buxton, he begins to handle colour with a mature confidence experimenting with opulent and dazzling juxtapositions new to the stained glass canon. The festive, affirmative luminosity is pushed even further in his radiant windows for Arata Isozaki's Lake Sagami Country Club, Yamanishi (1989), and distinguishes many of his subsequent schemes.

In the vast expanse of windows commissioned for the entrance hall of the Haus der Energie, Kassel, Germany (1992), Clarke has taken another radical step in re-examining the orthodox strategies for modifying light. Normally, stained glass reduces the transmission of light through a single, flat plane. It also encloses the interior architectural space, by, as it were, creating a 'curtain' which blocks out vision through the opening in the wall. The substitute window remains, while a less solid substance than the wall itself, a kind of barrier. At Kassel, Clarke's conception begins from a ground of 'white' or 'clear' glass (varying from transparent to translucent), which opens the interior out and creates intriguing spatial ambiguities in the relationship between interior and exterior, challenging our preconcep-

Cavendish Shopping Centre
(Buxton Thermal Baths), Derbyshire

New Synagogue, Darmstadt

tions of the function of a window. Onto this field of clear glass, 'ribbons' of colour, gathered into loosely rectangular forms, are floated (creating another ambiguity, of windows within windows). The trees and lawns outside are drawn into Clarke's composition, subverting the innate two-dimensionality of the window plane by introducing perspective effects. With deceptively simple means (almost minimal intervention), the interior of the building has been transformed and, simultaneously, intriguing relationships with exterior are suggested. At night, when the building is illuminated from within, common with the demands of many recent projects, the views of the windows from outside are equally compelling.

The organic, lyrical forms of the ribbon motifs at Kassel act as a counterpoint to the relatively austere geometry of the architecture; they respect the window spaces but render the interior a more humane and eventful environment. The 'disorder' that they represent does not signify destructiveness, but a poetic or spiritual polarity. The 'ribbons', which might be described alternatively as redolent of broad, painterly brush-strokes, scaled-up to an architectural format, appear to have originated in Clarke's paintings. Likewise, both the window motif and the preoccupation with spatial ambiguity have figured in his recent paintings. They recur, for example, in three oils from the 1993 series *Marks On A Blue Field*, in which clusters of window shapes hover over a deeply saturated blue field which is interrupted at one edge by a broad stroke of an opposing colour (pink, yellow and black, respectively); the interjecting swathe of colour occupies the foreground of the picture plane, beyond which the main activity appears to recede. Violating the equilibrium that has been established, these intrusions create the dualist tension that Clarke seeks in all of his work.

Certain motifs have preoccupied Clarke for long periods, but given that he has worked solely within the self-imposed constraints of a purely abstract vocabulary, the diversity of his visual forms is remarkable. While making a series of collages in New York he attempted to tear out cross shapes free-hand. Intrigued by the resulting vegetal forms, he developed them into organic elements which he calls *amorphs*, and which he uses to subvert the formal grid structure or repeated geometrical symbols of his paintings. The *amorphs* have also figured dramatically in several of his recent large-scale works in other media, including his vast windows for the arcade roof of the Victoria Quarter, Leeds (1990), and the rotunda and central square of The Spindles, Oldham (1993). In contrast with the restraint of the Kassel designs, his palette at Leeds and Oldham contains passages of an exuberant and celebratory richness. The *amorphs* have now become increasingly dominant, and their affinities are perhaps more accurately described as biological or cartographic, rather than vegetal. They recall, in almost seeming to evoke figurative associations, the cryptomorphic forms of Graham Sutherland. The stained glass of another Neo-Romantic painter, John Piper, is hinted at in the colour range of the Leeds and Oldham windows, in which Clarke alludes to the emblematic and heraldic aspects of ancient stained glass with an almost Fauve abandon and intensity. Sutherland is a painter whom he greatly admires, and Piper was a close friend for the last 17 years of his life. It is possible that some residual or unconscious inspiration from these essentially English painters found its way into these English commissions; at Oldham this would have been particularly appropriate since the windows celebrated their contemporary, the composer Sir William Walton. Certainly, Clarke has acknowledged that his designs were conceived as a 'homage', and his central square window includes a passage from the score of Walton's oratorio *Belshazzar's Feast*, and the programme with the initial page of the *Te Deum*, written for the coronation of Queen Elizabeth II in 1953.

Clarke has integrated his diverse inspirations into an ahistorical and wholly personal manner, in which his response to a given space is dictated by the aesthetic and functional requirements of the building. To illustrate the range of responses now at his command, we need only compare Leeds or Oldham with other recent projects. In contrast with their vibrant colour schemes, his series of predominantly blue-white panels for the intimately-scaled 'The Wall', Cibreo, Tokyo (1990), are the model of reticence. Similarly, the 13 windows for the New Synagogue, Darmstadt (1988), are skilfully arranged within a restricted palette to attain unity and to invite contemplativeness rather than celebration. Dr Suzanne Beeh-Lustenberger has described the 'interest and sensitivity' Clarke showed in his research before undertaking this project, and how he was 'deeply' moved by recent Jewish history.

For his part, Clarke is fulfilling his ambition to re-integrate art and architecture. Perhaps his most remarkable achievement is that his art has a resonance that is universal. His stained glass can be found in many different countries, in churches, synagogues and mosques, in shopping arcades, airports and office buildings, using a consistently architectural and spiritual language which transcends the specifics of its geographical location.

Architectural Artist

Kenneth Powell

Hôtel du Département des Bouche du Rhône,
Marseille (Model)

■ Perhaps the greatest omission in Brian Clarke's remarkable career so far is that he has never taught on any regular basis (though his appointment in 1993 as a visiting professor at London's Bartlett School of Architecture delighted him immeasurably). Clarke is a controversialist and theorist of substance in an area of the arts which, falling as it does into the divide between the 'fine' and 'applied' arts (a divide he resents and contests), has lacked a theoretical and conceptual base and positively fostered the bland, the repetitive and the platitudinous.

Mention 'public art' to Brian Clarke and you are likely to set him off on a line of argument which, though it is one he has often pursued, constantly causes him to question his own work, as well as that of others, and to urge a return to a way of working which was as familiar to the late Victorians as it was to the ancient Greeks but has got lost in the aftermath of the Modern movement. Clarke is no more reluctant to argue for a return to the past than were the great artists of the Renaissance, but he is equally a post-Modern artist, who has to live with the fruits, beneficial and malign, of modernism. Modernism has divorced art and architecture, yet the potential for the artist is greater than ever; glass, for example, is a fundamental element in modern architecture. Above all, Clarke passionately dismisses the idea that 'public art' – architectural art, as he would describe it – can exist in a vacuum, divorced from the dynamic influences which emerge not on the street or in the atrium of a building but in the artist's studio. This is why painting matters so much to Clarke. 'Painting is the reservoir of everything I do in the field of architecture,' he insists. Every significant artist has always known that 'art exists to break rules, defy conventions – that's the essence of it'. Precursors as varied as Giotto, Michelangelo, the Pre-Raphaelites and Matisse worked happily in the grandest and most intimate scale, but the essential quality of their work remained constant. One of the turning points in Clarke's early development was his first sight of Raphael's Vatican stanze, in colour pictures, in a book he saw at art school. 'I was knocked out. I realised that art had to work in a setting and that I had to work in the context of buildings.'

The key to Clarke's work lies in the ever-changing balance between the dynamism, energy and exploratory expressiveness of his painting, an art to which he constantly returns, and the world of architecture, simultaneously more pragmatic and formal – being a social and a commercial art – and yet profoundly visionary. It is not a matter of 'decorating' buildings: could anyone describe the Sistine ceiling or Matisse's work at St Paul de Vence as 'decoration'? He says, 'Art has to express emotion. It must be critical, radical, different . . . Decoration celebrates the commonplace, whereas art renders the commonplace sublime.'

Clarke's determination to reassert the role of the artist as a reactive force in creating architecture has led him to admire the work of William Morris and his Pre-Raphaelite collaborators. One of his favourite buildings, Alfred Waterhouse's Natural History Museum in London, could never have provided scope for Morris' talents. 'It's a great building,' says Clarke, 'but the art serves the architecture, it's part of the overall programme conceived entirely by the architect.' Clarke's own sympathies lie more with the Arts and Crafts approach practised by Victorian architects like Street, Webb and Sedding, who encouraged artists and craftsmen to express themselves within an architectural framework. Clarke's own education took place within an impeccably Arts and Crafts milieu. Admitted to Oldham School of Art at the age of 13, he studied bookbinding, pottery, photography and other 'applied' arts, as well as drawing and painting. Heraldry was the special interest of one teacher and Clarke was absorbed by it. At Burnley Art School, where Clarke proceeded after two years, a similarly broad approach prevailed. It was here that Clarke learned life drawing and began to be attracted to architecture: 'I considered becoming an architect, but was deterred by the idea that great "technical" skills were needed.' Nonetheless, the idea of working in buildings had become Clarke's prime motivation and he went on to study at North Devon College of Art because it was 'the place to do glass at the time'. Here he discovered the work of John Piper and Patrick Reyntiens and became obsessed with the Pre-Raphaelites. Piper was a particular influence and became a patron and a good friend to the young artist – 'his work was so obviously painterly – here was a really major artist who worked in glass,' explains Clarke.

Clarke might have developed in a more obviously English romantic direction had he not been exposed, at the tender age of 21, to the work of the modern German school of glass design. Pre-eminent among his new mentors was Johannes Schreiter – 'perhaps the greatest stained glass artist of all time,' Clarke believes. Schreiter, Ludwig Schaffrath, Georg Meistermann, Jochem Poensgen and others were products of the Bauhaus tradition. They worked in an abstract mode and found patrons in a Germany which had moved away from purely pictorial and narrative art. He remembers that, 'I was besotted . . . It was a revelation of how glass could move forward – and that didn't mean hideous blocks of epoxy resin like those I'd seen in Blackburn Cathedral.' Clarke's sojourn in Germany gave him the motivation he needed. He returned to England and began making glass. Within a year, he had glazed entire churches in his native Lancashire.

Given Clarke's interest in the Gothic Revival, his recurring interest in church liturgy (though he is a convinced agnostic) and his marriage to the daughter of an Anglican priest, a successful career in church work might have ensued. Clarke's hero Piper, a pioneer in the appreciation of the best Victorian glass, had executed masterly windows for the new cathedrals at Coventry and Liverpool. But Clarke quickly found ecclesiastical work impossible – 'there were endless arguments . . . I found the patrons weren't interested in the spiritual, just the literal.' He turned to painting to express himself and to renew his art. His interest in punk rock reflected his sheer exasperation with his patrons and his search for a new dynamic.

Clarke's career as an architectural artist began in earnest in the late seventies. His first major work, he believes, was the series of windows for the Olympus offices in Hamburg, completed in 1981. By this time Clarke had met and become friendly with his fellow Lancastrian – they were born not many miles apart – Norman Foster. 'We immediately began to bounce ideas off each other and have been doing so ever since,' Clarke says. Soon after, he met Arata Isozaki. A few years later, Clarke and Isozaki renewed their acquaintance and Isozaki suggested they might collaborate. Clarke had always admired Japanese art while Isozaki's richly layered architecture fuses Eastern and Western influences. The Lake Sagami Country Club, Yamanishi (1989), culminates in a circular rotunda which has a solemnity appropriate to a church or temple. Clarke says, 'the temptation was to merely embellish, but Isozaki wanted far more than that. He specifically did not want a religious gloom. He was very good at communicating the mood and the relationship of the colours to the spaces. Then he let me get on with it.' This is the sort of working relationship which Clarke values: a process of cross-fertilisation which arises most clearly when architect and artist can (as in this instance) work together from the beginning of a project. Clarke talks about his contribution as being, ideally, the antithesis of an architect's thesis. Result: a satisfying synthesis – the total work of art, the *Gesamtkunstwerk*, is the final objective. 'Harmony in the simplistic sense is not what I aim at,' he says, 'especially when the building is less than excellent. You have to fight buildings on occasions, especially the bad ones.' The most appropriate response to a building may be to attack it. There have been occasions when Clarke has worked in buildings he finds less than admirable, but, working with an artist-architect like Isozaki, collaboration is a matter of mutual understanding and communication.

Clarke describes Isozaki's architecture as 'meditative and exploratory'. In contrast, that of Will Alsop is 'all theatre and loud music – the grandeur only gradually emerges from the clamour'. Clarke's first collaboration with Alsop was on the Hôtel du Departement at Marseilles. 'Will deals in ideas. He's not at all reticent: he likes his buildings to perform – they're really events. And he is, of course, an enthusiastic painter.' Alsop says of Clarke: 'he understands the building process, he's architecturally minded. We wanted (and got) an art work which was part of the architecture but not dictated by it.' The task in hand was providing a huge wall of colour on the face of the building. Alsop had the idea of an expanse of blue. Clarke's work makes the actual cladding into a work of art; the technique being close to the faience popular with Edwardian architects. The result is an extraordinary combination of the functional and the artistic.

Alsop and Clarke have since collaborated on designs for the new CrossRail station at Paddington, where Alsop's concept is dramatically simple. A deep slit in the ground, marking the route of the new line, extends alongside the existing main-line station. It is expressed on the street as a long rectangle of glass, providing daylight to the platform level far below. Read from below, says Alsop, this is a railway cathedral; indeed, the height of the space from platforms to street equals that of Cologne Cathedral. The glass 'box' has been designed in close collaboration with Clarke. There was an obvious need to retain large areas of clear glass. In fact, the balance between plain and coloured glass is very carefully considered. Clarke describes the overall composition as 'episodic'. A particular emphasis is placed on the junction with Chilworth Street and Eastbourne Terrace, where the walker or driver faces a huge area of colour. 'It's a project to be experienced in many ways,' says Alsop, 'coming up the escalators, going down, looking up from the platform level.' Not the least of the vantage points is that of the air traveller. From high above, the station will read as an illuminated slash of colour.

Alsop is a highly innovative architect whose strong interest in sculpture – which he taught for a time at the St Martin's school –

informs his work and has allowed him to create a fluid architectural vocabulary of his own. He is the last architect to see the role of the artist as peripheral. 'The best artists to work with,' he believes, 'are those you don't regard as artists, just friends. The project is really a conversation between us.' But is not stained glass a remarkably conservative medium; at odds, even, with the expressive dynamism of the architecture? Alsop responds that, 'the point is the colour, the intensity – only stained glass can achieve it. You could, I suppose, remove the leading – bolt blocks of colour to sheets of clear glass. But that is a decision I leave to Brian.'

The 'conversation' with the architect is a critical matter for Brian Clarke. He wants to retain the right to be disturbing, disconcerting, questioning. If there is one example of the art of stained glass which embodies those qualities for him it is the great east window at York Minster – 'far greater than any at Chartres,' he says – made by the Coventry glazier John Thornton c1408. It is a work which is as shocking, albeit within a medieval Christian framework, as anything in modern art. It is neither subservient to the late Gothic architecture of the Minster nor at odds with it. Thornton worked within the architectural context, using it for his own ends, 'wrestling' with the building. Clarke describes the results as 'awesome'.

Brian Clarke's early work – for example, in the Lancashire churches – has a free, flowing quality ('lyrical', in Peter Cook's mind) which probably reflects the early influence of Piper and which, for all the tautness and rigour of the later glass, has never entirely vanished. (Indeed, it shows signs of re-emerging strongly in the 1990s.) Clarke's maturity has coincided with remarkable developments in architecture, with a new spirit of invention and freedom which has shocked some conventional Modernists of the older generation. Jan Kaplicky and Amanda Levete, who previously worked with Foster and Richard Rogers but now constitute the London partnership Future Systems, design forms which echo nature but are still dependent on late twentieth-century technology. Kaplicky and Levete have worked on two projects with Clarke, both unexecuted, but they are close collaborators, part of the circle which informs his view of architecture. Future Systems first worked with Clarke on the competition entry (1992) for the Ministry of the Environment building in Hamburg, the 'Glass Dune'. This huge glazed 'wave' (or 'boomerang'?) is typically sculptural and three dimensional. 'I think Brian was surprised by the 3D nature of our scheme,' says Kaplicky, 'but together we made something totally integrated.' Kaplicky admits to a nagging concern about the conventional nature of stained glass: 'if we had built Hamburg, we'd have wanted to challenge Brian, to see what could be done with a different technique. The possibilities are surely enormous.'

Clarke is far from averse to experimentation, but responds with a defence of lead as a frame for glass: 'the lines animate the whole – in general, there isn't a substitute.' He warmed to Future Systems despite, perhaps because of, the apparent 'irrationality' of their work. (Was Le Corbusier of Ronchamp or the Foster of Willis Faber an irrationalist?) The sheer beauty of the scheme impressed him and the project developed as a close collaboration, with architectural, structural and artistic ideas developing together to create a totality. Engineer Tony Hunt created an elegant and functional frame for the glass. 'We lived it for four months,' says Clarke of the Hamburg

Crossrail, Paddington (Model)

scheme. A specimen panel of Clarke's glass adorns the London studio of Future Systems, a token, one hopes, of future collaborations.

Clarke's desire to work with architects and engineers to create total works of art might seem to marry uncomfortably with commission to work in existing buildings. Yet Victorian and Edwardian buildings of character seem to draw a positive response from him. The former Lavers & Barraud workshop in Endell Street, Covent Garden, is one of them; appropriately, it was a significant Victorian stained glass manufactory. As part of an office conversion, Clarke designed a window for the top floor conference room. Set in a Gothic frame, the glass is rigorously gridded, a deep blue in hue, with inset frames of white glass. Only the sinuous tendrils which invade the frame disturb the severe orderliness of the scheme. Clarke's glass reflects his careful study of Lavers & Barraud's own palette. The far larger area (8,000 square feet) of glass at the Victoria Quarter shopping centre in Leeds (1990) made Clarke revive this approach. The scheme involved glazing over an entire street lined with buildings designed by the ebullient Edwardian architect Frank Matcham. Clarke's collaborator was Derby architect Derek Latham, with whom he has already worked on the refurbishment of Paxton's Thermal Baths in the spa town of Buxton (1984-87). 'I looked at the ornamental glass, Matcham himself designed. I had specimens scanned and reduced to colour constituents and then restricted my palette to Matcham's own.' Clarke was constantly aware of the complexity and decorative richness of the setting – 'a complex multivalent space, redolent with symbols and imagery, requires a complex response,' he says. The area to be glazed was 400 feet long and there were practical considerations. A high degree of natural light was needed if the space was not to be made oppressive. Similarly, a framework of plain glass helped to emphasise the unity of the street itself.

Brian Clarke refers to 'the happy marriage of the Edwardian sense of circumstance and the more clearly focused and linear vision of our own time,' in the Leeds scheme. The colour range of the glass is certainly extremely rich, even lavish, moving from green through a rich blue to a quite violent orange over the centre of the arcade (for such the street has become), where it links to the existing County Arcade, also the work of Matcham and included in the overall Latham concept. In short, Clarke gave himself free rein in Leeds. The effect is stunning, though the intensity of the glass and the lyrical delicacy of its detailing makes Latham's roof look a little heavy. The 'Gothic' references in the steelwork are a little too obvious and not very appropriate. Matcham was the most un-Gothic of architects. Yet it is hard not to see the new 'arcade' as a sort of cathedral of shopping. Yet the doubts about the architecture remain: what could Norman Foster have done here?

Clarke compares the Leeds glass with the exactly contemporary scheme installed at the Cibreo restaurant in Nichi Azabu, Tokyo (1990). The building was a new one, designed by the British architect Nigel Coates, with interiors by Naoki Iijima. The commission was for the glazing of one wall of the interior, a total of 512 square feet of glass to be set within a rigidly rectangular framework (though the wall is actually canted, not straight). A serene effect was wanted, emphasising the poised quality of the interior. 'It demanded the most restrained colouration and form,' says Clarke, 'and could hardly have been a more different situation to that in Leeds'. Clarke broke the scheme along the grid of the window frames, with the bottom third filled with a trellis of deep blue. Above, the glass is opalescent, almost clear but with a bluish tinge, but invaded by curving, natural shapes and, more forcefully, by a great rectangle of brilliant red. Clarke goes so far as to reinforce and defer to the architect – then he asserts himself forcefully – goes on the offensive, 'attacks' the architecture. Clarke is an ardent admirer of Japanese art and architecture, but it disturbs him that stained glass (often Victorian glass recycled from redundant churches in Britain) is often used in Japan as trivial decoration for bars and night clubs. 'The Japanese don't really understand stained glass,' he says. 'They think of my work as something else – an architectural filter or something of that sort.' Yet only in Japan perhaps could the business of eating be reconciled with work of such gravity as Clarke designed for the Cibreo. The completed work has true dignity, perhaps even solemnity, and a certain spiritual calm.

Clarke's early experiences with church commissions have been related. His detachment from conventional Christianity seems total, while retaining a spiritual view of the world; however, he has worked happily within a religious tradition which is not his own, that of Judaism. The synagogue at Darmstadt, designed by Alfred Jacoby, was completed in 1988; the 50th anniversary of the infamous 'Kristallnacht', when persecution of Germany's Jews began in earnest. Judaism is a conservative faith. There is little scope for liturgical innovation. The essential elements of a synagogue are constant. There must be an Ark, containing the sacred Torah scrolls, and a bimah, the elevated platform from which the scrolls are read. The separation of men and women in the congregation generally demands the use of galleries. The emphasis on reading in the synagogue services makes good lighting a necessity.

Jacoby's Darmstadt synagogue has a typically conventional basilican plan with a shallow apse to contain the Ark. Clarke was asked to produce 13 windows in all, ten along the 'nave' of the building, two flanking the Ark and a glazed half-dome above the Ark. The artist had to ensure good natural lighting and equally reconcile his ideas with the fairly rigid format of the building, for example, would the galleries not wreck any attempt at overall treatment of the side walls? Clarke's windows were based on the lattice which owes a clear debt to Charles Rennie Mackintosh, but equally is in tune with the work of Mondrian, an artist who has had a persistent influence on his work. That gives them their overall artistic discipline and ties them into Jacoby's formal – Post-Modern, in truth – architecture. But the Darmstadt synagogue is full of symbolism, traditions, memories. The calm quiet at the heart of the Jewish faith is there, but there is also a memory of the horror which the building commemorates. The essence of calmness finds expression in a predominance of blue glass, but is balanced by a run of brilliant, fire coloured windows. (The interest in flames, invading a calm frame of lines, appears in Clarke's paintings of this period, for example *Composition in Red* or the disturbing *A Quiet Tribute to my Friend Gertrude Higgins*.) The Heidelberg synagogue, also the work of Alfred Jacoby and formally opened in 1994, has led Clarke to experiment with new glass making techniques.

Clarke talks of the 'intellectual ping-pong game' which he plays:

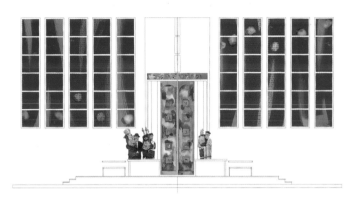

Heidelberg Synagogue (Design)

Paul McCartney World Tour

on one side is his painting, on the other his architectural art. The two are at odds, but without either one there is no game at all. Water-colour is a medium which Clarke uses relatively rarely. (He used it when working up his designs for the Future Systems Hamburg Scheme.) Its special qualities might seem peripheral to the matter of stained glass design. For the Heidelberg commission – ten windows, each six metres high – Clarke actually dispensed with conventional leading. He had the idea of 'pools' of watercolour piercing areas of solid blue colour. (The effect provided enormous difficulties for Clarke's manufacturer, Mayer of Munich.) Clarke also wished to incorporate panels of Hebrew texts into the glass, a technique familiar to the Victorians but unusual in modern glass (though Clarke's revered Schreiter had used it for his stunning series of windows designed for the church of the Holy Spirit in Heidelberg, but never actually installed there). The result is one of the most technically accomplished and, artistically, most ambitious of Clarke's schemes.

The Victorians, who Brian Clarke, by and large, reveres for their revival of the art of stained glass, despised Georgian glass. Joshua Reynolds' work in the chapel of New College Oxford was often quoted in the last century as the nadir of the art, an insult to the medieval architecture around it. Clarke has come to see merit in the Georgian approach: 'painting on glass,' as it has been described. 'It is anti-Gothic,' he admits. But at Heidelberg it seemed the right way to incorporate the particular character he sought. Clarke has an ability to bring together moods and ways of working and yet achieve an overall unity. The texts in these windows are presented in a way which, he concedes, reflect the influence of Pop Art.

It is many years since Clarke made his own glass – transporting it, to one church in Lancashire, on the local bus! But his interest in the production of glass is still strong and his relationship with his makers is a lively one. 'In my youth, the British Society of Master Glass Painters was dominant,' he says. 'The ethos was that of the last gasp of the Arts and Crafts – if you didn't make your own glass, you were thought immoral, a cheat.' But craft techniques, worthy and time-hallowed as they are, have a limited relevance when a commission is as big as, say, that for Leeds. The artist has to concentrate on being an artist. He learned from John Piper that it is more important to paint than to try to be a craftsman. 'I design with a view to the process of manufacture. The glass is made to match my colours exactly. The texture, the degree of opacity, everything has to be as I see it. Distinguishing the role of the artist from that of the craftsman does not in any way demean the latter . . . I can make glass if I want to, but I have come to see my role as something different'.

Stained glass is an art form which Clarke currently dominates. But his notion of *Gesamtkunstwerk* embraces other media. The Heidelberg synagogue has an Ark which he has embellished with mosaic, a material which increasingly fascinates him. 'Most recent mosaic work is simply daft, limp, shallow,' he says. 'But look at the profundity of Ravenna.' Textile design is another area into which he has been making striking forays. But the core of Clarke's achievement lies in the interaction between painting and glass, as applied to architecture. (The rock and ballet sets – the most spectacular of them executed for the 1993 McCartney World Tour – are, in truth, transient architecture.)

Two recent projects illustrate very vividly the range of Clarke's work in glass. The Spindles shopping centre in Oldham, Brian Clarke's home town, is not a great work of architecture. It is typical, not exceptional, but it does no harm to a town which lost out to its neighbours because of lack of investment. 'Oldham,' says Clarke, 'lost a lot of its character long ago, though I have fond memories of the place in the sixties.' Clarke was commissioned to produce two very large windows as central features of the two 'courts' of the development, around 2,500 square feet and 3,000 square feet in area, respectively. He had the idea that the glass might commemorate a famous son of the town, the composer Sir William Walton. 'We used to declaim Walton's *facades* when I was at art school in Bideford,' Clarke recalls.

The glass in the central square at the Spindles incorporates flowing foliage-like forms against a deep blue background. Only in one area does the usual Clarke latticework make an appearance. Instead, there are literal mementoes of William Walton's life – a letter he wrote when a chorister in Oxford, part of the score for *Belshazzar's Feast* and the cover of his *Te Deum* written for the 1953 coronation. The glass evokes the spirit of his music. The rotunda – an octagonal space – contains gridded panels which make up a subtle programme of colour, from deep blue through to white.

Clarke talks about 'attacking' buildings, 'fighting' them. 'The last thing an artist should be is reticent,' he says. 'You have to be prepared to run counter to the building. Only rarely can you work with the building. You know, I actually enjoy working in bad buildings sometimes: making something of them.' The Spindles is hardly a bad building. But it is a distinctly ordinary building. Clarke uses it as a canvas, a frame which he has the task of filling, and creates a memorable monument for a town which has few monuments.

The Haus der Energie at Kassel (1992) is the headquarters of a major energy generating company designed by local architects Bieling & Bieling in association with the leading German practice von Gerkan, Marg & Partners. It is a building of serious quality in a mode which is characteristic of late twentieth-century Germany, with 'high tech' elements yet, equally, a monumentality which recalls the late work of James Stirling. The site is on the edge of town, and the 500 staff who work there enjoy a remarkably 'green' environment.

Clarke's initial commission was for a glazed ceiling to the board room. 'On reflection, they decided that this was rather elitist,' says Clarke. The building had already been designed and the architects were concerned that the insertion of coloured glass would compromise its transparency. The designs for glass in the lofty entrance hall and dining room (which is a continuation of the latter at first floor level) had to take these views into account. He therefore decided to break down the commission into two distinct areas, rather than imposing a single theme across the elevation. For the restaurant, he wanted to create 'pools of atmosphere', distinct and characterful areas within the large room with an ambience of their own. ('Rather like Eduardo Paolozzi's enclosure at the Caprice in London'.) The colours could complement the mood of someone dining there, or he could choose to sit by a clear window and enjoy the excellent view. 'I've been there and people have come up to me and told me how much they love the place; surprising for an office canteen!'

One of the objectives of the architect's designs was to make the building look 'open' and unbureaucratic from outside, as well as a pleasant place for those inside it. The company was concerned that Brian Clarke's designs for the entrance hall might create a private, even introspective atmosphere. 'I simply cut out all the background colour,' says Clarke. The design was reduced to a series of strips of colour set in lead, with areas of opalescent colour occasionally invading the clear sheets. Result: an extremely fluid effect, light and elusive, yet the coloured glass verticalises and monumentalises what could have been a relatively routine space. Clarke is extremely happy with the results. 'It's the first time I've ever signed a window'.

Kassel marks a high point in Clarke's career to date. Itself amongst his best works, it comes at a time when he is experimenting, rethinking his art – working on more projects than at any time before. There have been periods when Clarke has painted little, but he has been actively at work recently.

Norman Foster wrote: 'Surely modern architecture can with the right kind of collaboration go beyond the "tokenism" of art in architecture and lead to a genuine liaison in the spirit of past ages. Such future possibilities will only be realised when there is a shared language of awareness between patrons, architects and artists.' However, Foster adds, 'it requires a particular kind of thinking for an artist to work in architecture if the quest is to go beyond the professional partnership into a shared endeavour . . . Clarke has that approach.'

Without question, the greatest project which Clarke did not execute was his collaboration with Foster at Stansted Airport, an unquestioned icon of post-war British architecture. There were ideas of great strips of colour along the glazed elevations of the terminal building; however, it never happened, though Clarke was commissioned to design a tower of stained glass as a focal point for the airport's catering area. 'Foster,' says Clarke, 'has a total view of art. Stansted is still the most enjoyable thing I've done. But the original idea would have been my *magnum opus*, I'm sure.' Given Clarke's friendship with Foster, there must be some hope that the two men will work together again before long – and on a big scale.

'I used to stand on a hill near Preston,' says Clarke, 'when I was in my early 20s and it gave me such pleasure to think that every church I could see had a window by me.' Clarke does not spend much time in Lancashire now, but it gives him pleasure to see that early work. His place is now on the world stage. He has done more than anyone to restate the place of the artist in the making of architecture, not as a decorator but as a creative force. Just turned 40 years of age, Clarke has a clear role in the new architecture which is emerging as the twentieth century ends.

Drawing on Architecture

Brian Clarke

There was a time for me when making paintings was a means of somehow proving myself, of describing how well I was able to make the paint do what I wanted. There are exceptions, but on the whole my paintings provided me with a satisfaction analogous to the contentment felt by a signwriter with the power to contour a perfect Roman character. Occasionally, and by this I mean about 20 times in as many years, and usually (it seemed) by accident, a work unrelated to this pleasure would thunder through my efficient filtering system of reticence and trepidation. These paintings were always, in one way or another, characterised by their 'drawn' quality. When I look back over my paintings it is to these few that I can most comfortably return.

Any attempt to come close to an appreciation of the language of my paintings necessitates some appreciation of architecture. In one sense it is true to say that my paintings exist in independent isolation of my architectural activities, but it would create a false impression to leave it at that. All articulate artists develop a vocabulary and language of their own. It is formed out of aesthetic sense (taste) and out of the shuddering chaos of personal experience. It is a language given its poetic value by loss and by victory, by affection and by the death of those we love. Its syntax and structure are formed out of sensitivity to the external material world. Interior suffering and epiphany made coherent through the aegis of exterior physical sensibility. This language is nearly always characterised by particular obsessions. It takes very little time to identify that my particular obsessions are largely architectural.

In the paintings, these interests are not restricted or forced in any specific direction by the needs of a building. They can float, uninhibited, uninterrupted and unreliant on three-dimensional issues. It is as if the architectural language I employ in trying to give sense to volume, space, mass and rhythm is released from having to make sense. This liberation results in an exuberant and (for me) very physical experience. In no longer having to deliver a narrative my words (marks) become instantly something in themselves. In literature I think the writing of Gertrude Stein is similar. Words become liberated of their meaning and therefore free to mean something new or at least unexpected. Everything becomes less certain, less confined.

In my architectural work my strengths, for what they are worth, are created out of the very restrictions that might inhibit my paintings. It is my response to spatial problems and issues that tighten and focus my statements in buildings. Though the paintings are not entirely innocent of these conditions they are for the most part unconcerned with them. Marks, gestures, textures and colours that in a building would have to answer to numerous masters in order to make a worthwhile contribution to a space are suddenly free to find their own lovers, their own lives. The journeys they make in this situation are often very productive. They are the agencies through which are delivered new forms, new juxtapositions and new compositions. Surprising counterpoints, intervals and confrontations take place across the freedom of the canvas field. As often as not these discoveries find their way into my stained glass and mosaics. Although some paintings begin life with a loose 'stratagem' or 'design' they almost always transmogrify early into something quite different.

When I paint, an overwhelming sensation of freedom animates

my decisions. When I move from painting to working in architecture, oddly enough, the same sense of freedom still pertains. This 'ping-pong' from one to the other is a vital aspect of my work and peace of mind. I could not imagine working in either discipline in isolation.

Anybody who has ever drawn with a pencil in an effort to convey an idea, however abstruse or abstract, knows how profound the feeling of satisfaction is when the drawn marks result in an efficient or successful analogue of the thought that provoked the act. When that thought is conceptual rather than literal and the nature of the line and the temperature of the colour are more important than the figurative simulacrum, the degree of satisfaction is multiplied.

At the time of writing, my paintings tend to be produced in a strict pattern. They begin by covering the stark white canvas with thin washes of burnt sienna oil colour. These washes, as far as I understand them, have two functions. First, they remove from the picture plane the paralysing virginity of the white rectangle, taking away the sense of terror that always accompanies the first mark. And second, the different levels of wash create an illusion of depth of field and imply a foreground, a middle distance and a dark spatial continuum. The spatial quality of these watery brush-strokes I find comforting and ancient. It is odd, therefore, that the next step in the current process, as soon as drying is complete, is to paint over the whole of this swirling panorama with thick, dark, unthinned oil paint. Usually, a deep ultramarine or permanent blue. At first sight this impasto colour appears so dark that it looks black. Only as the eyes adjust to the 40-50mm brush-strokes does the warm hue of the deep ultramarine become visible. At this stage, some remnants, memories of the swell and splutter of the burnt sienna, still bubble up through the more ordered blue layer of colour. These are consigned to history as soon as the ultramarine is touch dry and ready for a second, third and fourth layer of gradually lighter hues to be applied. At present, these subsequent layers are all blue; but in the past greens, reds, oranges and greys have also been used. Each layer reveals only a little of the one beneath and by the sixth or seventh skin a rich vibrant field of often quite thick impasto is formed. This is the complex plane that I feel relaxed about with regard to drawing, and whether the marks are made with a brush, a pencil, an oil stick or my fingers, the act I perform is drawing.

At no time in any of the work I do am I as unconscious, as lost in the act, as I am when I execute the drawing stage. As I said, there usually exists a sketch or collage that suggests a composition. On the whole, because this is my nature, this sketch is usually quite resolved and self-contained, and I always intend to simply follow my own instructions and translate the scale drawing to its full size. I begin with this earnest intention and after a few minutes always forget it and get lost in a forest of white characters and symbols. My hand and arm become agitated by their inefficiency, and the events that follow curiously seem to be orchestrated more by a stomach nervousness than a cerebral control. This period, depending on the size and complexity of the painting, can last from half-an-hour to several hours. During this time I am conscious of conflicts, minor battles and disagreements. Of calm, tranquil open space and of the despair of loneliness. An exuberant optimism occasionally animates the lines and calls for more colour, for punctuations into the membrane of blue or

sap, or leaf green or vermillion. Faces rush by as do buildings, and often architectural plans and the unclear recollection of light falling on stone or metal. Shafts of liquid light pushed through the filter of stained glass, flowing over brass or marble, over brick or tiles often come to mind. The marks that time and nature scratch into the palms of hands and into the faces of buildings, but most of all my little crosses and circles, my tiny squares and nervous lines become something entirely their own and begin to make their own unique sense. I can speak about them as if they are nothing to do with me, for apart from these cloudy sensations and fleeting momentary half experiences the time I spend making these marks is lost to me. I am left with a sensation of having been a semiconductor.

I suppose about one-half of the paintings I make find their way out of the studio and the other half are painted over. I particularly like overpainting finished works as it gives me such rich grounds to play with. It is always instantly obvious if the enterprise has been successful, or not. At times I overwork, overstate or exaggerate gestures, at times the compositions are too conventional or lazy and at times fanciful or over complex. The paintings that I most enjoy are those which seem to advance 'the' argument, though I am never quite sure what the argument is. I paint in 'lumps' of time intensely for two weeks or a month and then go immediately, fired by the experience, into designing stained glass, or at the moment, mosaics. The intensity of the experience makes architecture entirely comprehensible.

My most successful architectural work is always produced immediately after a period of painting. I cannot pretend to understand why, but the paintings are a means for me to come to terms with the contradictions and confrontations that occur in buildings. Massing versus layering, weight versus buoyancy, rigidity versus fluidity. Stillness versus movement, light and dark, soft and hard. The terrifying monologue that recites the complexities and contradictions in architecture is briefly no longer at all bewildering.

The Clinical Research Building and Hammersmith Cancer Centre

Hammersmith Hospital, London

In collaboration with architects Future Systems, who were commissioned to design the interior of the Cancer Centre, Brian Clarke has designed a stained glass rooflight for the main waiting area and stained glass screens for the two glazed walls of the entrance hall. In both cases, Clarke's glass forms an inner coloured membrane, suspended in a horizontal plane below the external rooflight glazing and vertically annotating and concealing the outside world, through the entrance hall screens.

The colours and the types of glass for the windows were especially chosen to help induce a feeling of calm and restfulness.

The photograph shows the collage designs for the entrance hall windows.

Size:
Rooflight: *58 sq metres (624 sq feet)*
Screens: *67 sq metres (721 sq feet)*
1993

Marks on a Blue Field (A Child Waits), 1993. Oil on canvas, 190 x 150cm (75" x 59")

Marks on a Blue Field (Marseille), 1993. Oil on canvas, 200 x 150cm (79" x 59")

Hastings (For a Child of Five), 1994. Oil on canvas, 183 x 305cm (72" x 120")

Marks on a Blue Field (Recollection of a Lost Child), 1993. Oil on canvas, 190 x 150cm (75" x 59")

Elegy to Lost Time, 1994. Oil on canvas, 200 x 450cm (79" x 177")

Marks on a Blue Field (Rajasthan), 1993. Oil on canvas, 153 x 107cm (60" x 42")

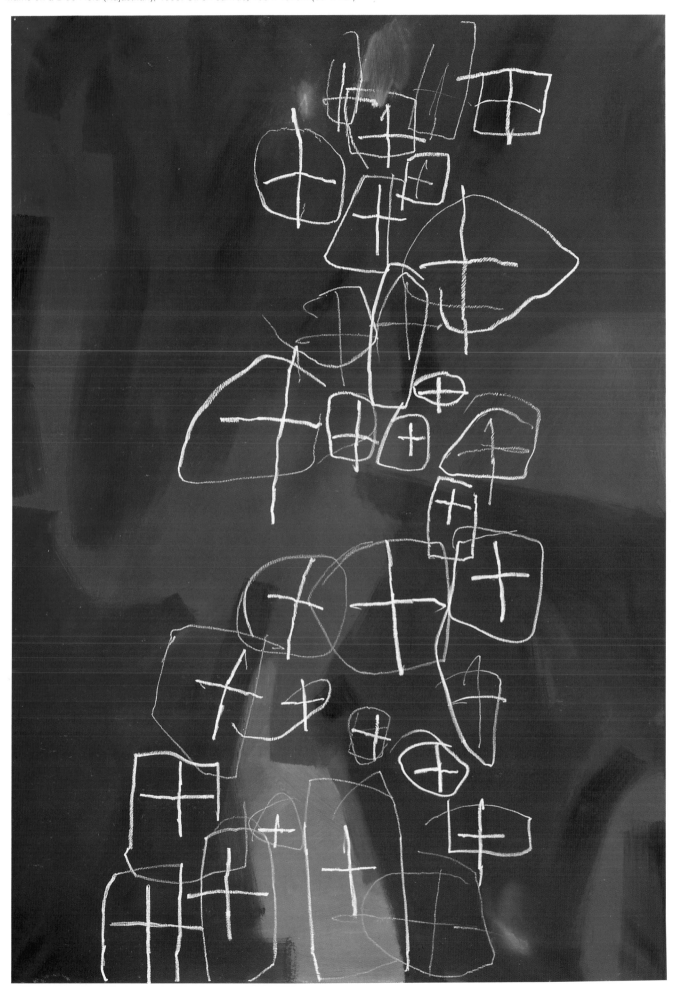

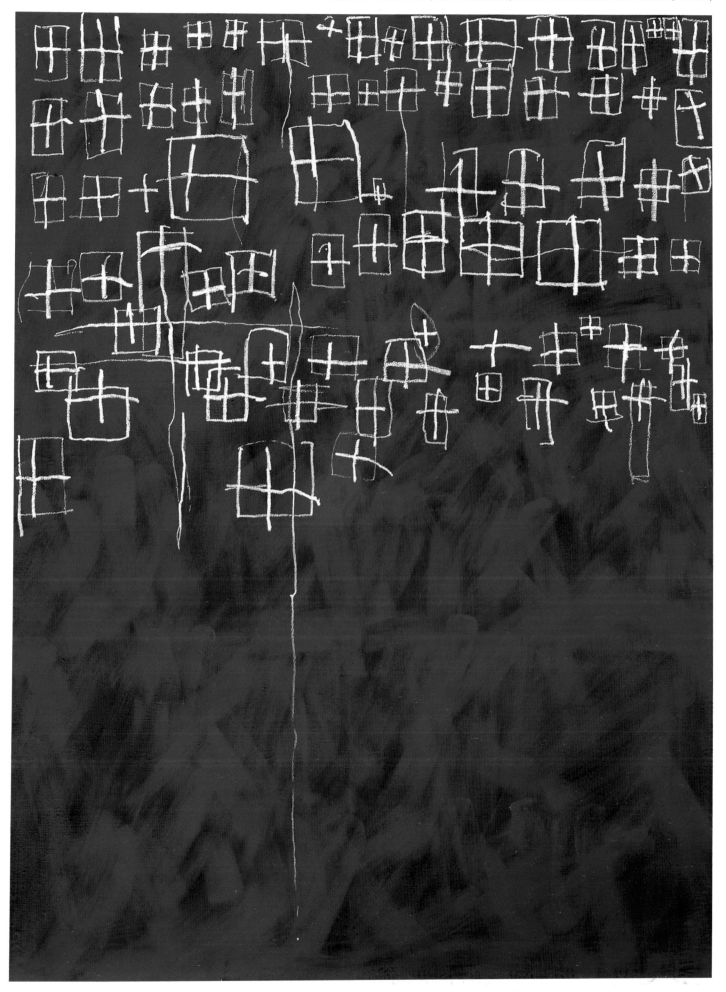

Marks on a Blue Field (Romantic Landscape), 1992. Oil on canvas, 250 x 428cm (98" x 169")

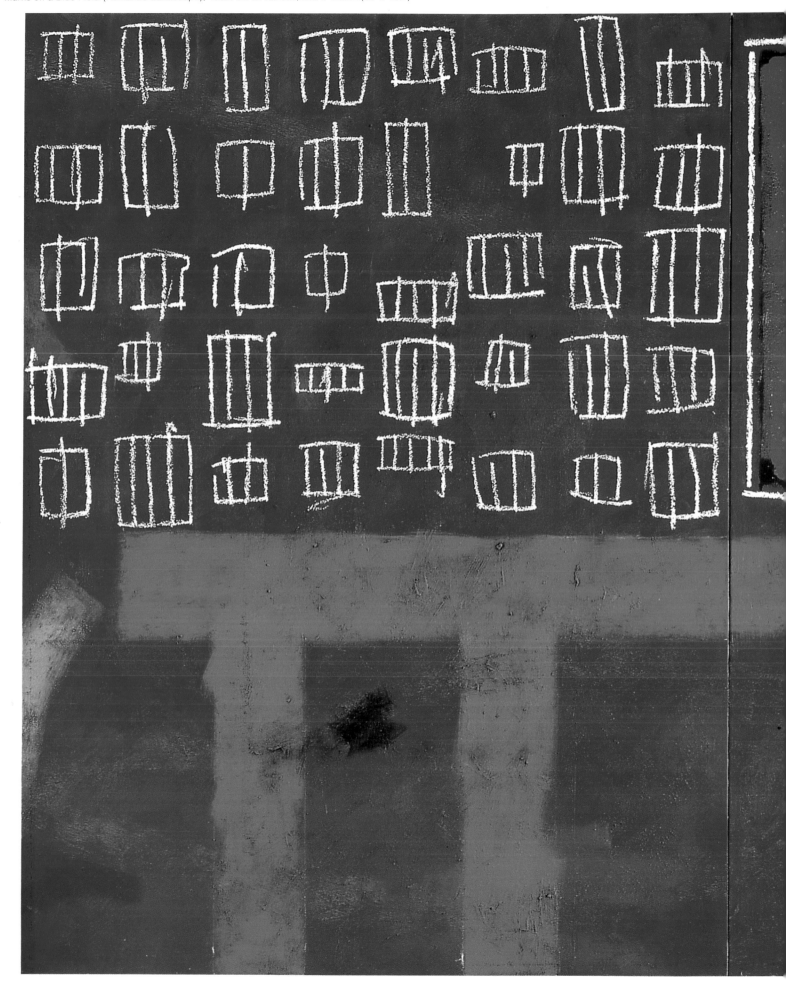

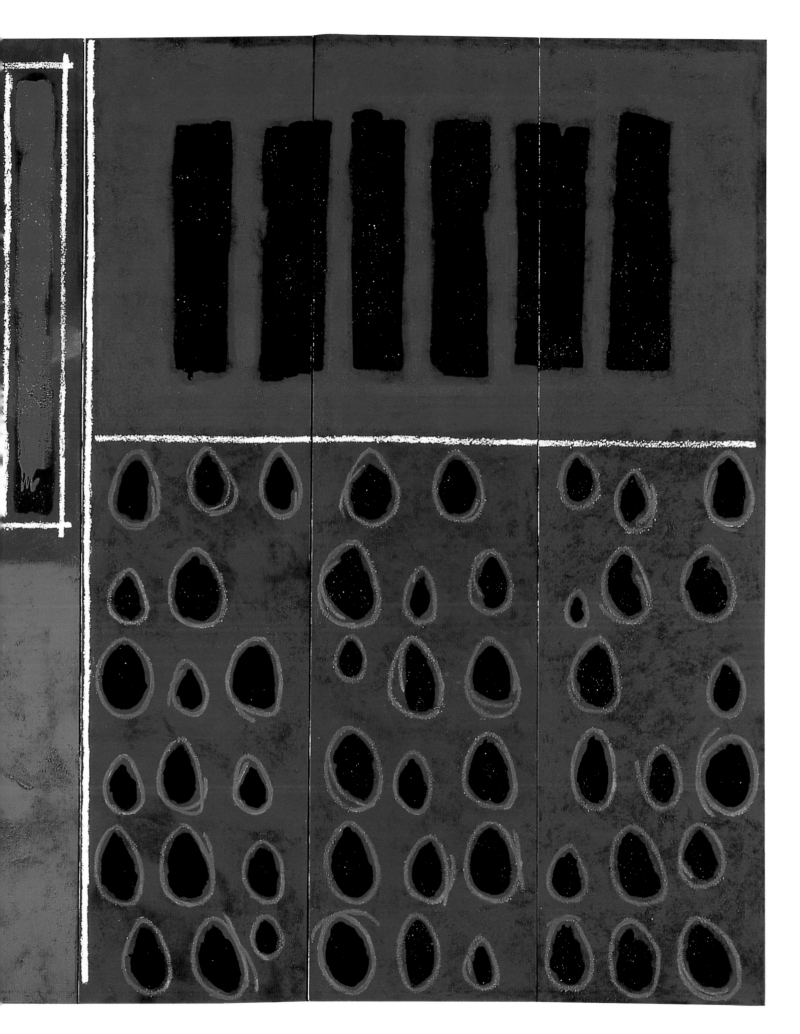

Marks on a Blue Field (All Things That Rise), 1993. Oil on canvas, 101 x 75.5cm (40" x 30")

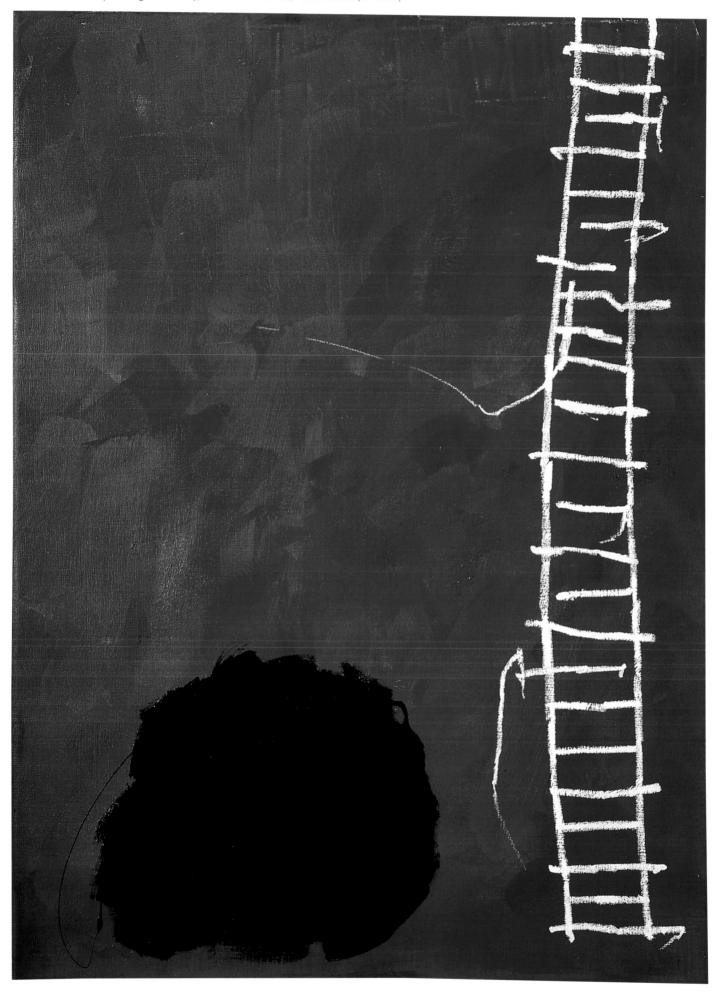

Marks on a Blue Field (Vice into Virtue), 1993. Oil on canvas, 200 x 200cm (79" x 79")

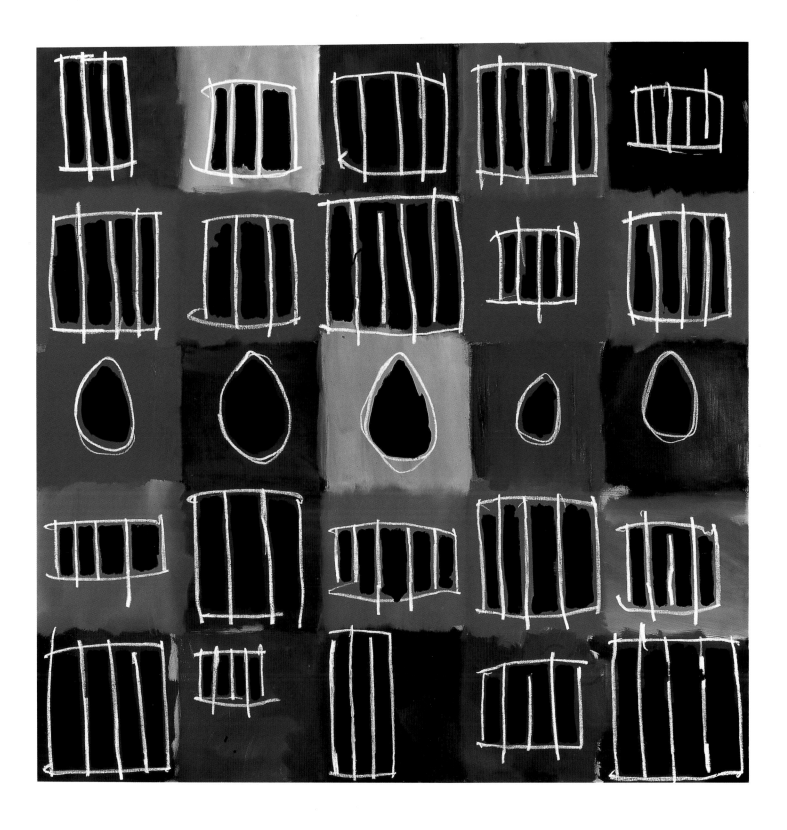

Marks on a Blue Field (Horseman Pass By), 1993. Oil on canvas 150 x 200cm (59" x 79")

Marks on a Blue Field (Love Him More), 1993. Oil on canvas, 122 x 170cm (48" x 67")

Lake Sagami Country Club

Lake Sagami, Yuzurihara,Yamanishi, Japan

Every element in the design of these complex windows exists by virtue of relation and reaction to features of the building. The lantern tower is visible from a great distance and by night becomes a powerful beacon. It is internally illuminated by a lighting system, designed by Isozaki, which falls from the centre of the tower and rotates slowly transforming the cylindrical form into a glowing and radiant corposant.

The original design of the building incorporated a pyramidical structure later abandoned, but Clarke retained the reference to this in the form of a blue directional triangle intersecting a field of olive green in his skylight composition. At other points, the 'nave' of the building and the owners' apartment (formed in glass bricks) are hinted at by formal geometric reference in the skylight forms and colours.

Architect: *Arata Isozaki & Associates*
Client: *Yamada Corporation*
Project size: *350 sq metres (3767 sq feet)*
Installed: *1989*

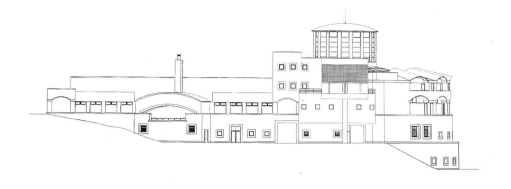

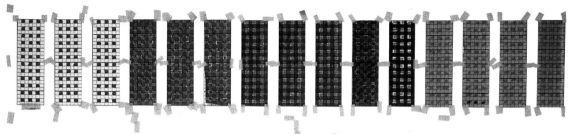

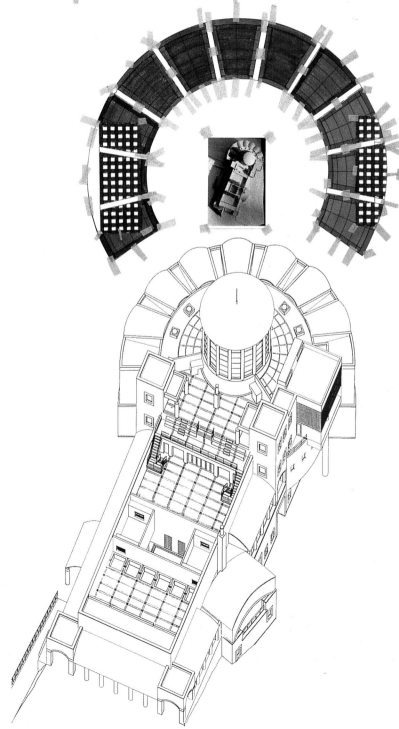

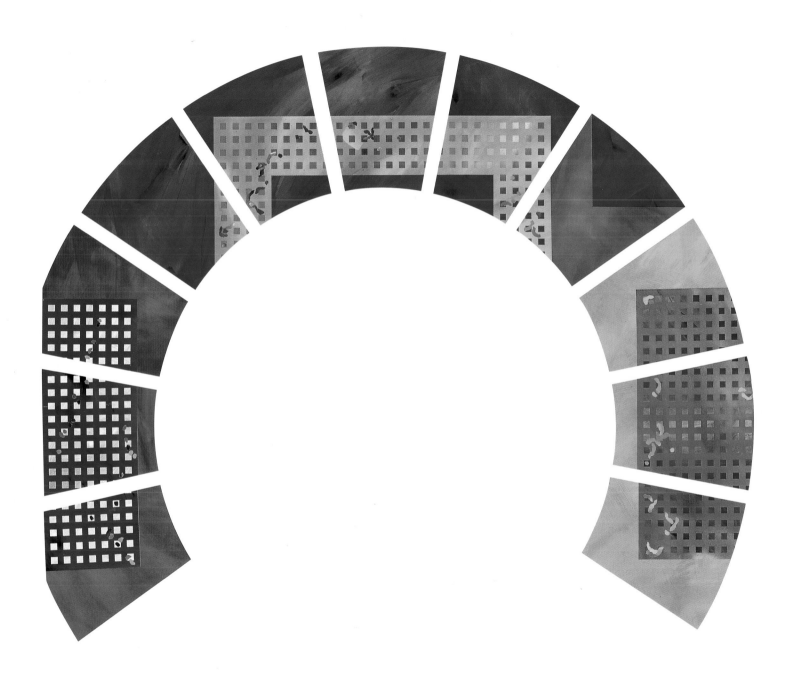

The Victoria Quarter

Leeds, Yorkshire, England

Victoria Street in the city centre of Leeds forms the main circulation route between Briggate and Vicar Lane. It is also the central artery of a labyrinth of turn-of-the-century arcades which form the old heart of the city's shopping centre. The Prudential Insurance Company, through their investment manager Ray Chan, commissioned Clarke to work with Stewart Hodgkinson of Derek Latham & Company to produce a stained glass roof to span the entire street. It was decided to leave the lower eaves in clear glass so as not to disturb Matcham's original polychromatic glazed brickwork, and the initial concept of enclosing the two end facades in stained glass was abandoned in favour of light central areas of coloured glass.

Architect: *Frank Matcham*
Architect to the conversion: *Derek Latham & Company*
Client: *Prudential Insurance Company*
Project size: *747 sq metres (8041 sq feet)*
Installed: *1989*

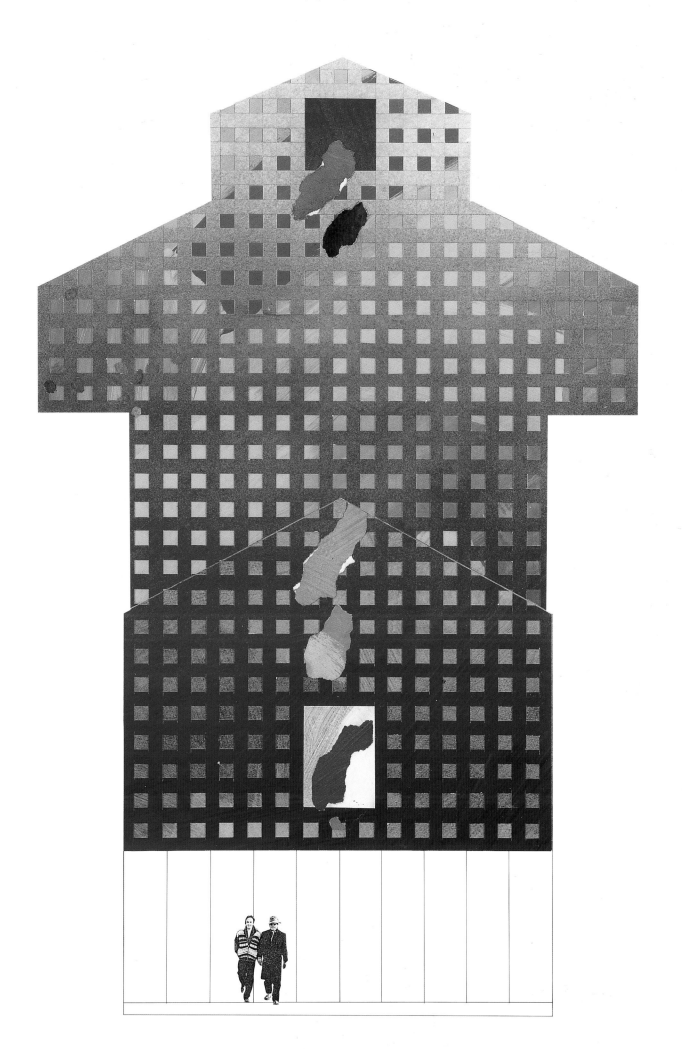

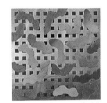

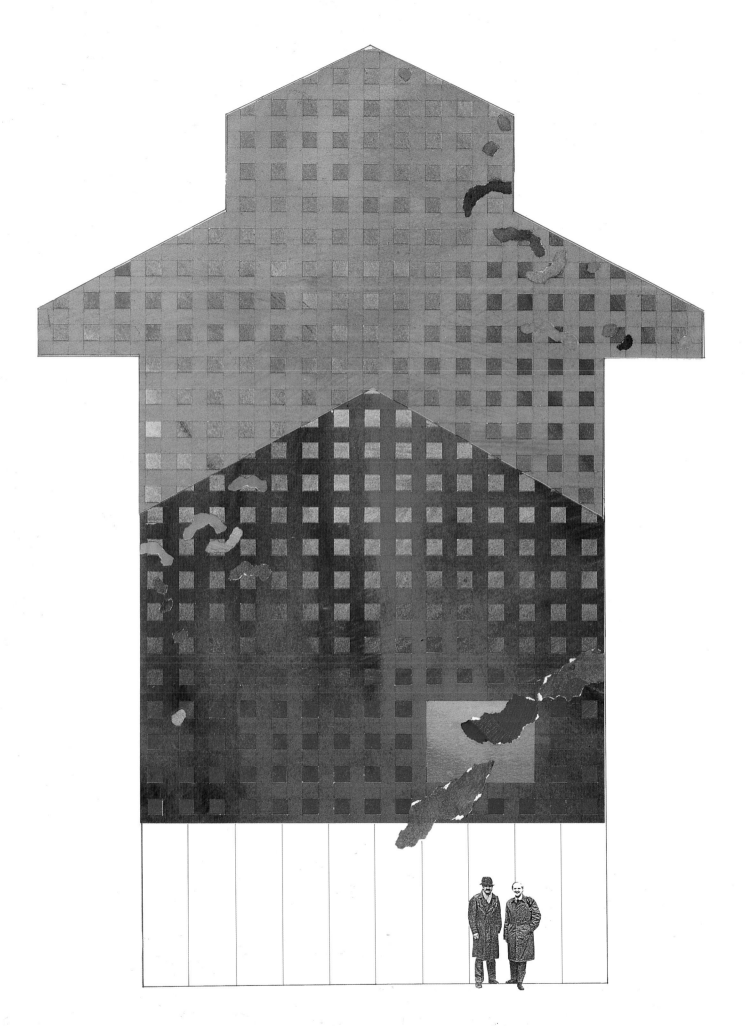

Cibreo: 'The Wall'

Nishi Azabu, Tokyo, Japan

The top floor of this five-storey building in Tokyo, in comparison to most of Clarke's other projects of recent date, is very intimate in scale. It represents a most convincing example of the artist's ability to produce highly restrained and passive compositions when the situation demands it. Responding to the limited space, Clarke designed a work delicate and quiet in colouration, interrupted by very controlled forms that recall his earlier painterly interest in Japanese screen painting and calligraphy. The frame of the window conceals adaptable lighting that makes it possible to illuminate the screen by night so that the composition has an 18-hour working day.

Architect: *Nigel Coates*
Interior architect: *Naoki Iijima*
Client: *Mitsutomo Co Ltd*
Project size: *48 sq metres (517 sq feet)*
Installed: *1990*

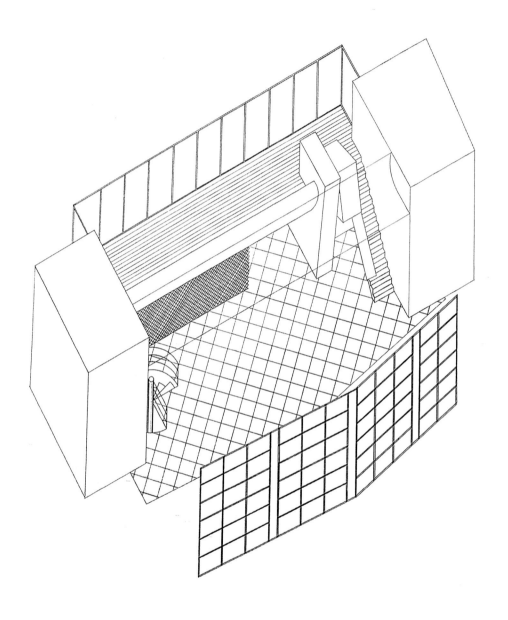

Oldham Town Centre: 'The Spindles'

Oldham, Lancashire, England

A series of three interrelated roof lights in stained glass connecting and spanning the main public areas of this retail shopping centre. Originally conceived as a series of five roof lights and later modified, reducing to three. The design for the central square incorporates specific reference to the music of Sir William Walton (born, like Clarke, in Oldham). These elements include musical scores from *Belshazzar's Feast*, the initial programme page of the *Te Deum* written in 1953 for the coronation of Queen Elizabeth II and a highly magnified facsimile of a letter written by the composer when he was a chorister at Christ Church, Oxford.

The 'small mall' was motivated by the *Orb and Sceptre Coronation March* and marks a break away from the amorphic elements of the other compositions towards a more painterly abstraction disrupting the grid. Unusually for Clarke, this area has been fabricated largely in opalescent and 'opak' glass rather than transparent colour.

Architect: *Bernard Engle*
Client: *Burwood House Group plc*
Project size: *628 sq metres (6760 sq feet)*
Installed: *1993*

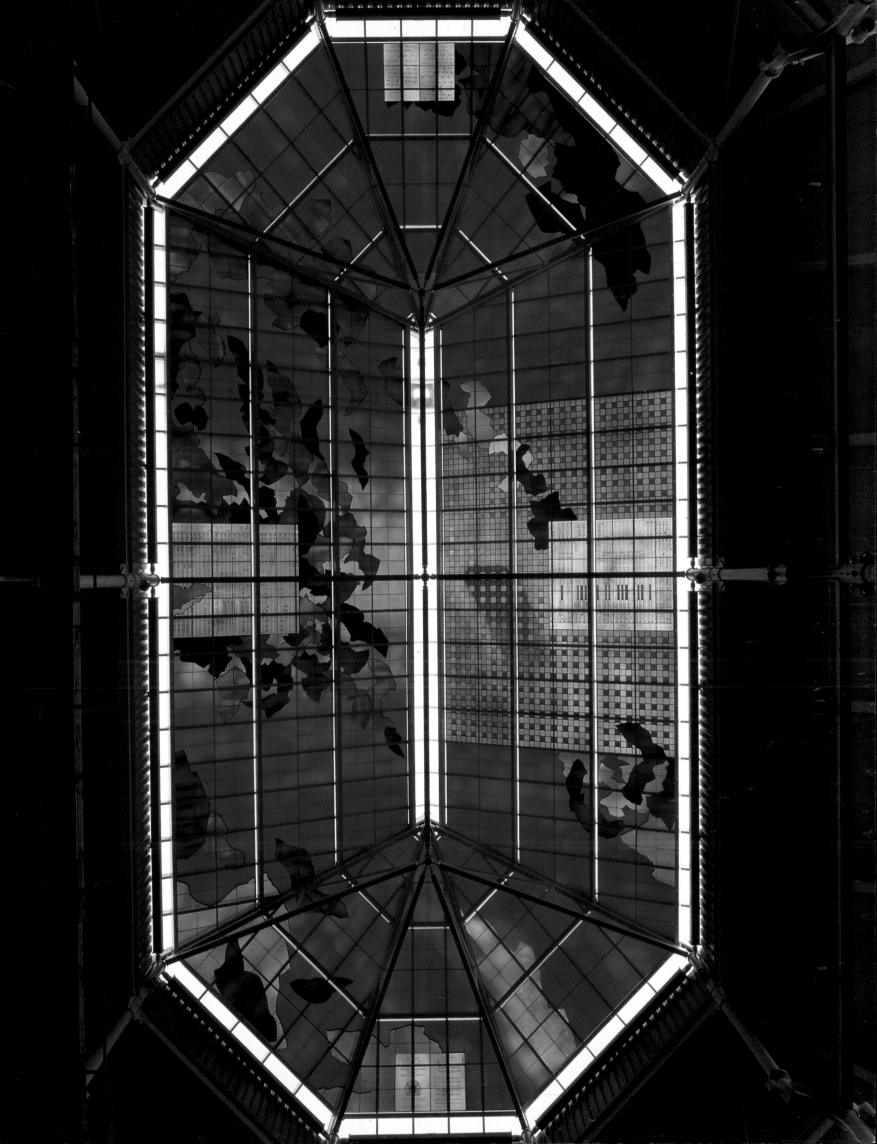

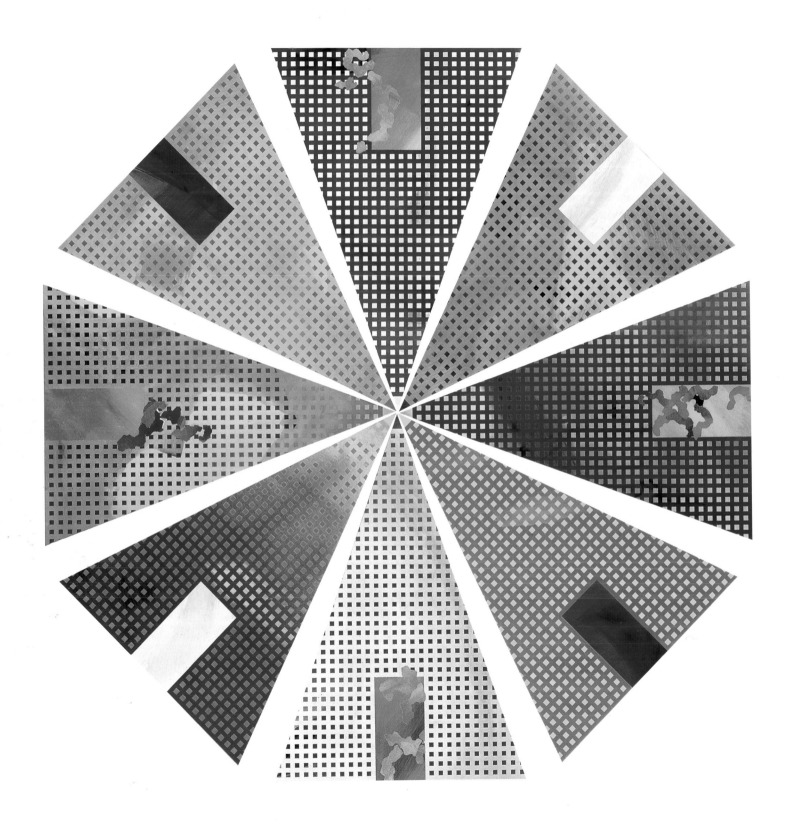

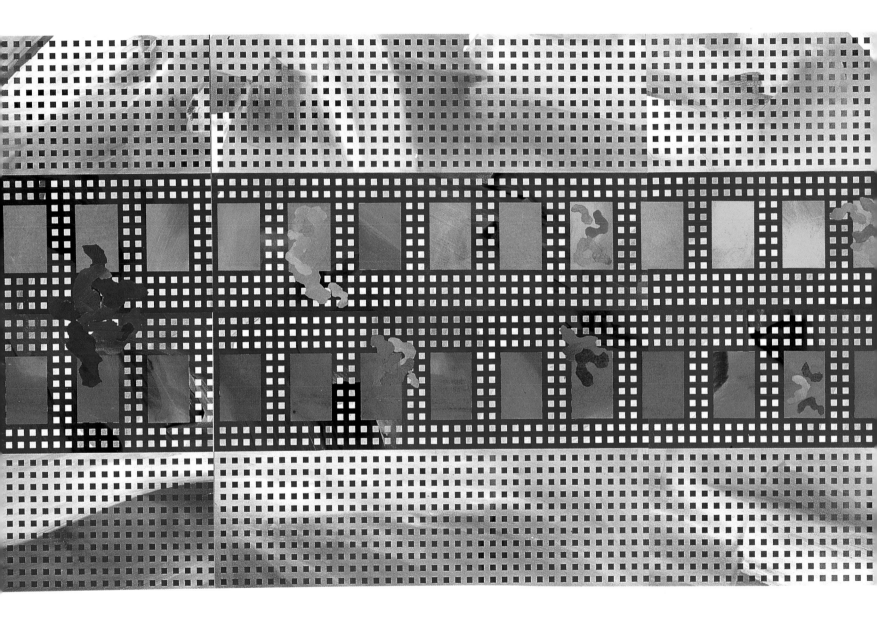

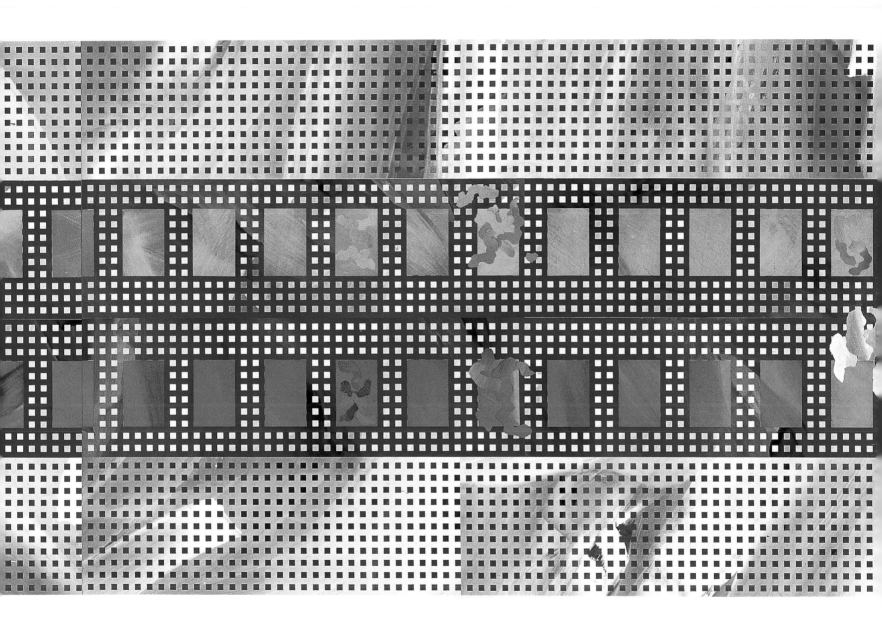

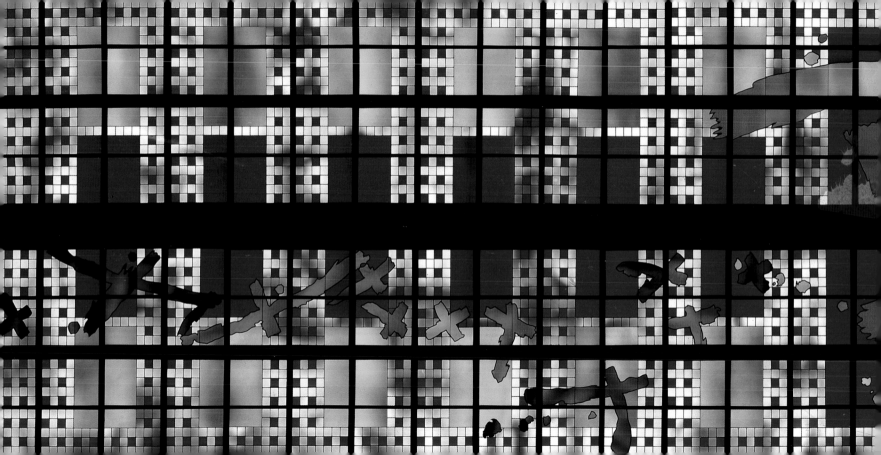

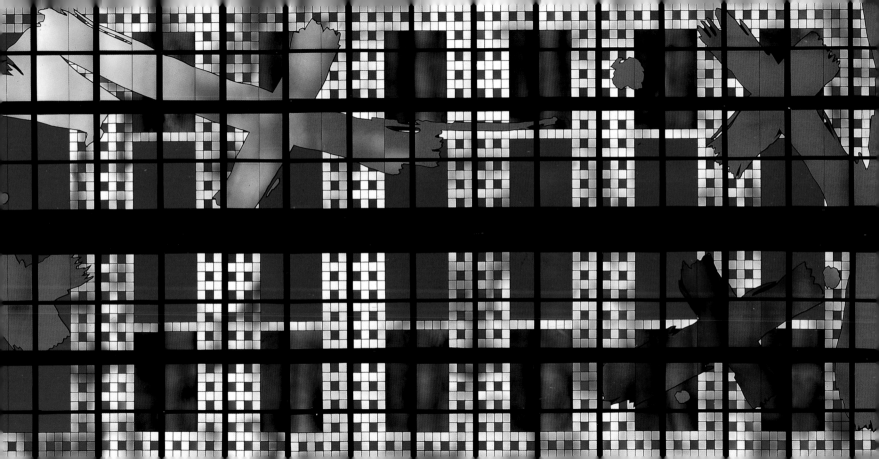

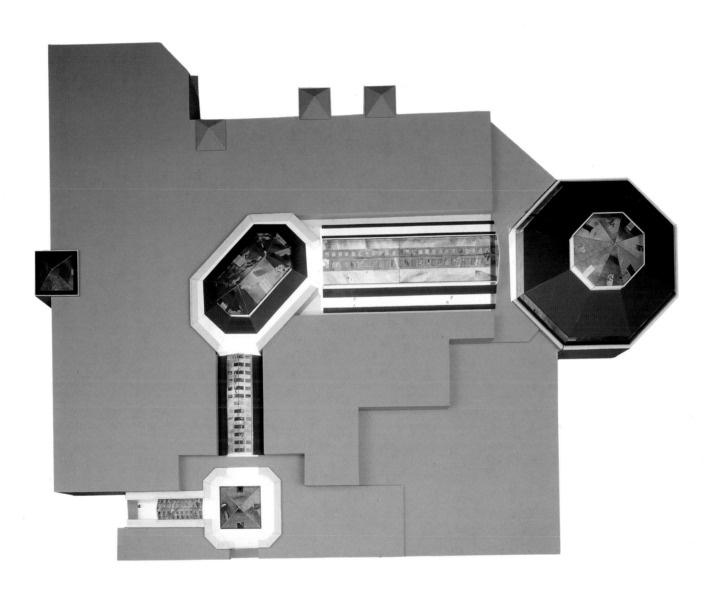

London Airport, Stansted

Stansted, Essex, England

The original proposal for Stansted involved two dramatic sequences of stained glass panels along the east and west walls of the terminal building. These forty-four grid-based panels were developed by the artist in collaboration with Sir Norman Foster and Spencer de Grey as a contrapuntal development of 'perforations into the white opaque membrane of the building'. In their own turn, Clarke's own grids were subsequently disturbed by apparently random 'amorphs' of colour. This was probably the first time in the development of the medium of stained glass that computer-generated projections have been used by the artist. For complex technical reasons it proved impossible to incorporate this scheme, but Clarke later produced a project for the 'Food Court' in Stansted installing two complementary back-lit glass friezes and a tower of stained glass.

The friezes opposite each other and in their shared geometry echo the structure of Foster's building. The centre of the court is presided over by a four-sided six metre high tower of stained glass illuminated from within. As the airport has grown the tower has sadly been removed to 'allow greater flow of traffic through the space'. It is currently being relocated in the terminal building.

Architect: *Sir Norman Foster and Partners*
Client: *British Airports Authority*
Project size: *136 sq metres (1464 sq feet)*
Installed: *1991*

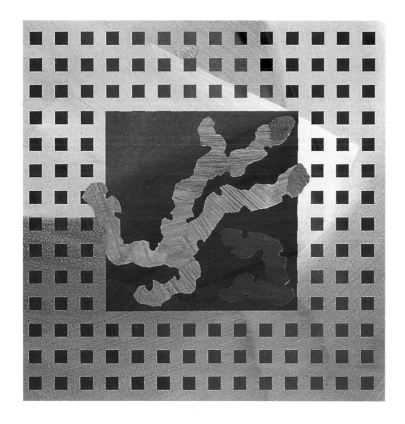

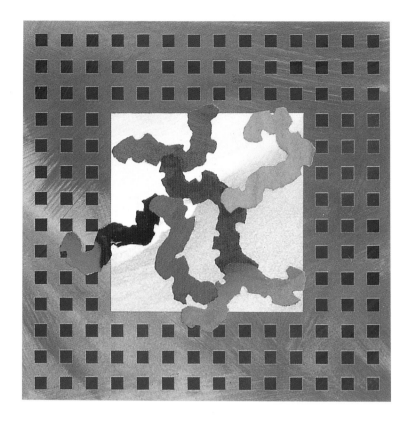
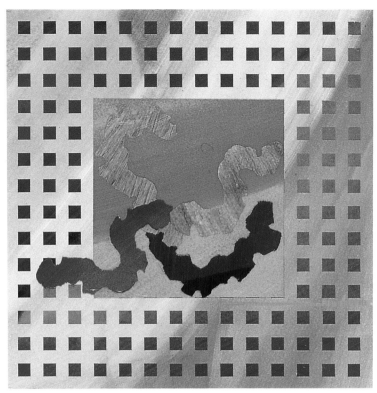
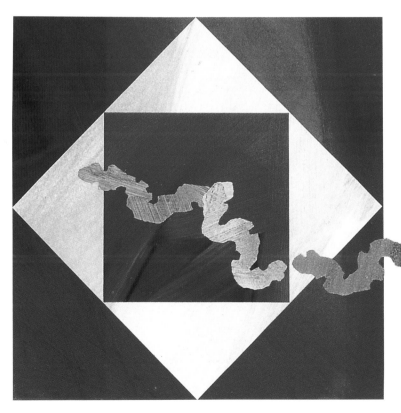

100 New Bridge Street

London, England

This building lying at the junction of New Bridge Street and Fleet Street nearby to St Pauls Cathedral forms part of an extensive city development by developer Stuart Lipton.

The scheme incorporates a stained glass entrance screen and canopy on the New Bridge Street facade of the building. By day, the entrance glass is illuminated by natural light and is at its most potent from within. The canopy is also visible by natural light from the pavement level. By night, internal illumination brings the two elements of the scheme jointly alive delivering an energy and atmosphere to the streetscape it sadly lacked before. It has now become an affectionate landmark in the City of London used as an evening meeting point and directional event.

The glass is itself animated by 'ribbons' of colour, and white also contains small points of onyx and agate which breaks up the flow of more linear passages.

Architect: *RHWL*
Client: *Rosehaugh Stanhope*
Project size: *80 sq metres (861 sq feet)*
Installed: *1992*

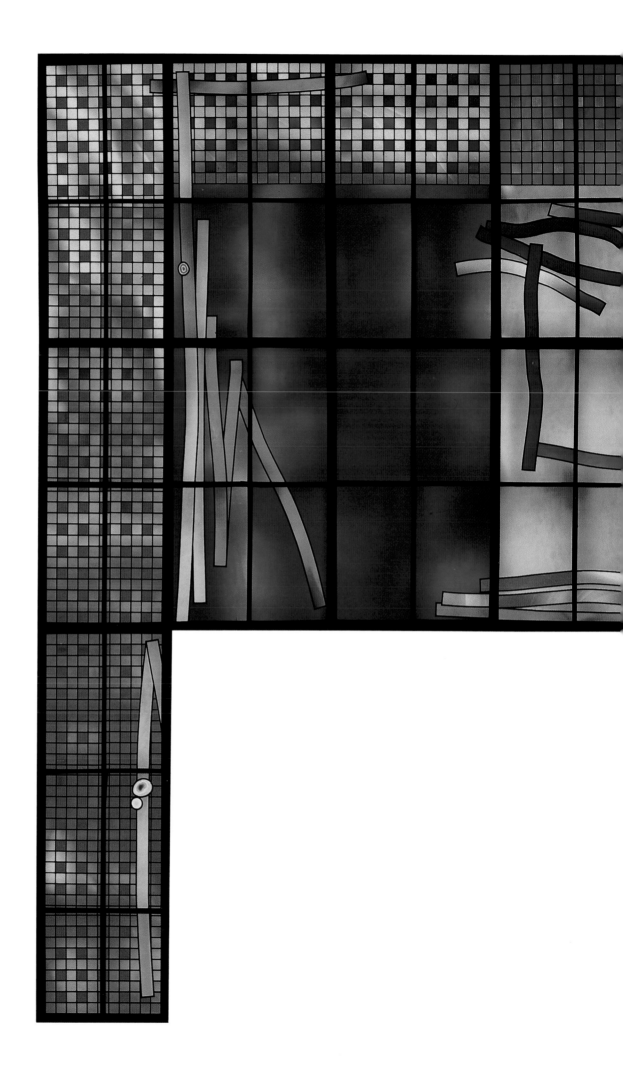

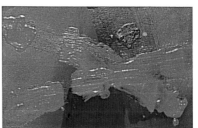

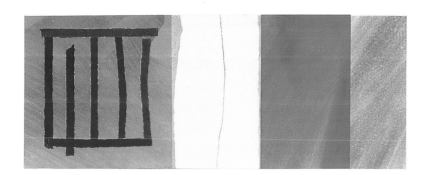

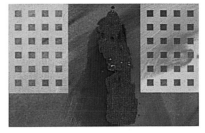

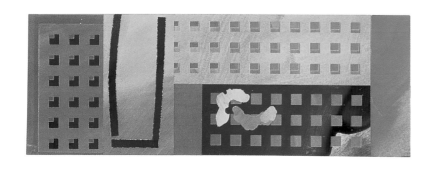

The Carmelite

Carmelite Street, London

A series of eleven stained glass windows which punctuate, with pillars of colour, the exterior walls of the Victoria Embankment and the Carmelite street elevations of the building.

Inside the building, Brian Clarke was commissioned to produce five 90 feet tall textile wall hangings. Each reflects and enhances the mood of the interior of the building in an abstract narrative to a crescendo of colour in the rear atrium space. As well as providing an extraordinary sense of warmth and atmosphere, these tapestries produce a substantial acoustical improvement in this lofty central atrium.

Architect: *Trehearne & Norman*
Client: *Associated Newspapers Ltd*
Project size: *Glass – 8 sq metres (86 sq feet) in total*
Tapestry – 320 sq metres (3444 sq feet) in total
Installed: *1992*

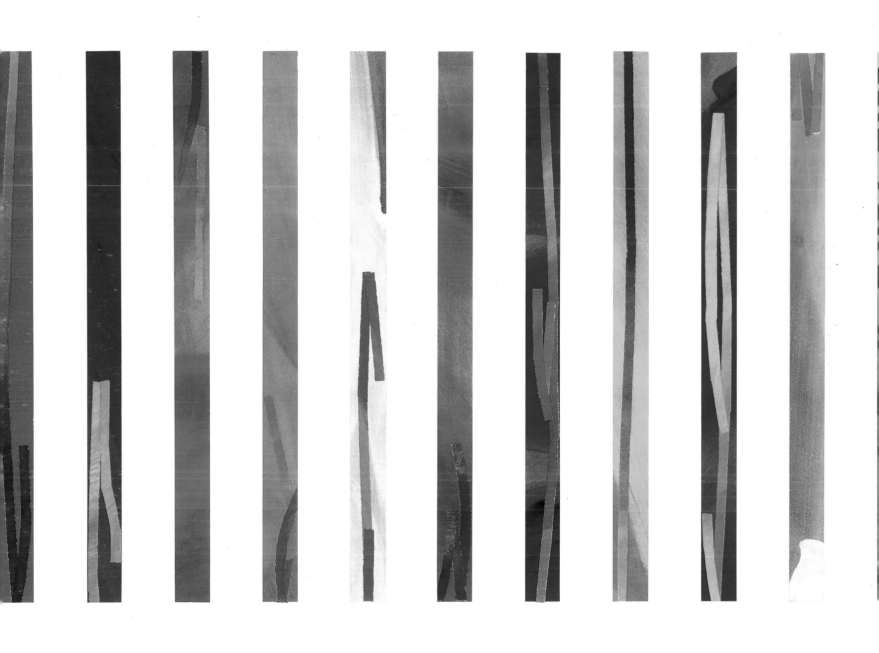

The Glass Dune

Hamburg, Germany

Future Systems, the architectural practice of Jan Kaplicky and Amanda Levete who came to prominence for the Bibliothèque Nationale de France design, asked Brian Clarke to cooperate with them on this competition entry. The project was never built but represents a most exciting potential for collaboration of the highest order. The new forms created by Future Systems in their particular blend of organic Modernism provoked an altogether different approach from Clarke. Taking the so called 'boomerang' plan of the building (designed to be a response to the energy efficient and non-polluting technologies) Clarke constructed an internal 'skin of art' that spans the internal plane of glazing. He felt that the bank of escalators climbing through the offices were an important 'animation' when viewed from outside and that the view through the wall of glass was equally important for visitors to the building as they used these stairs. Accordingly, he left the central area entirely clear save for two great ribbons of orange and yellow that dart across the space forming a bridge between the halves and lower down skirting the entrance, teasing the public in.

The atrial heart of the building would therefore become a dramatic south facing space enlivened by the movement of people horizontally and vertically and by the passage of light through this complex and delicate skin of colour. All the floors open on to this atrium which also contains shops, restaurants and terrace. All the office floors would directly access this animated and light filled space.

Clarke has now completed another design with Future Systems for the Hammersmith Hospital in London.

Architect: *Future Systems*
Client: *Ministry of the Environment*
Project size: *1,100 sq metres (11,840 sq feet)*
Designed: *1992* (Joint invited competition entry)

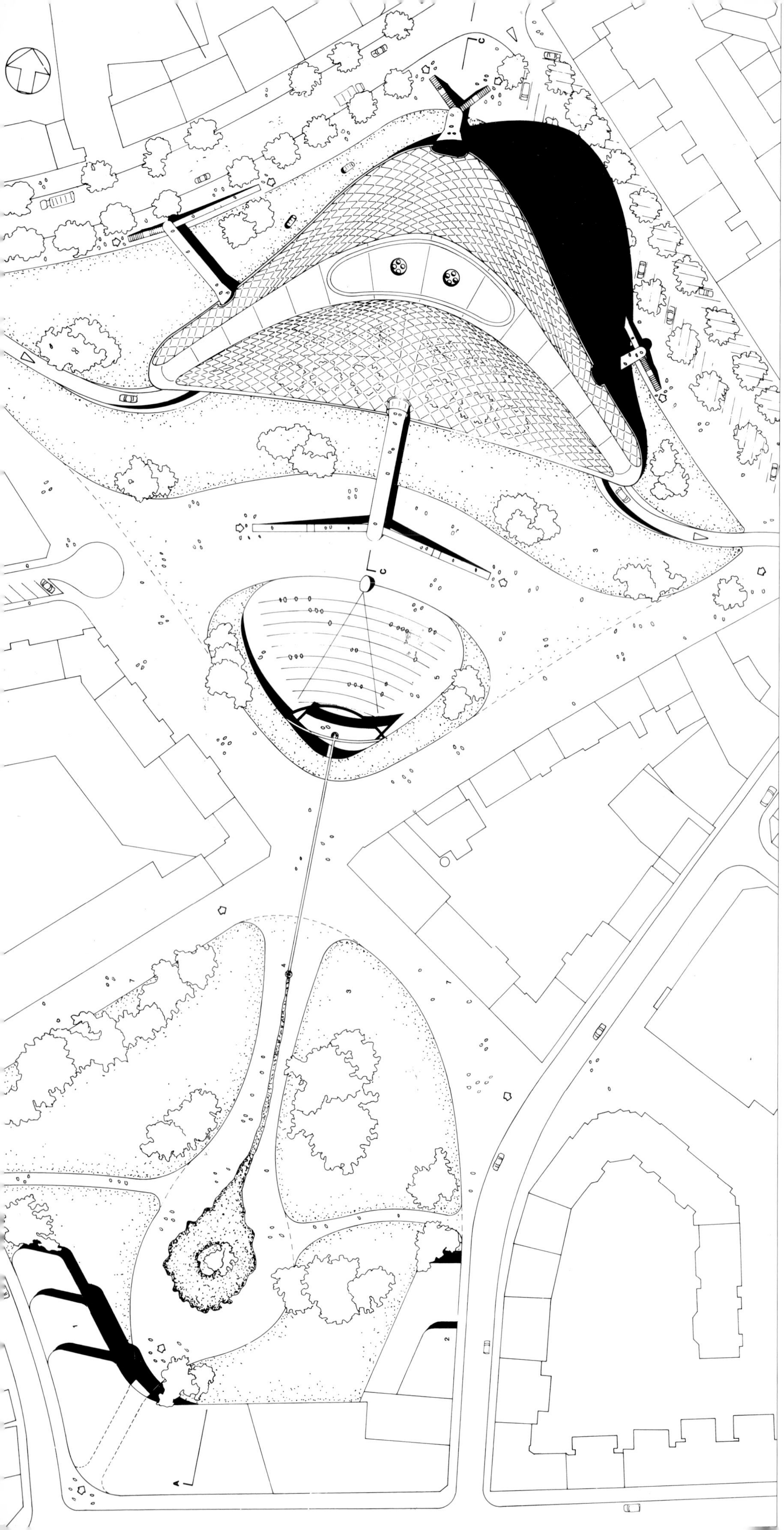

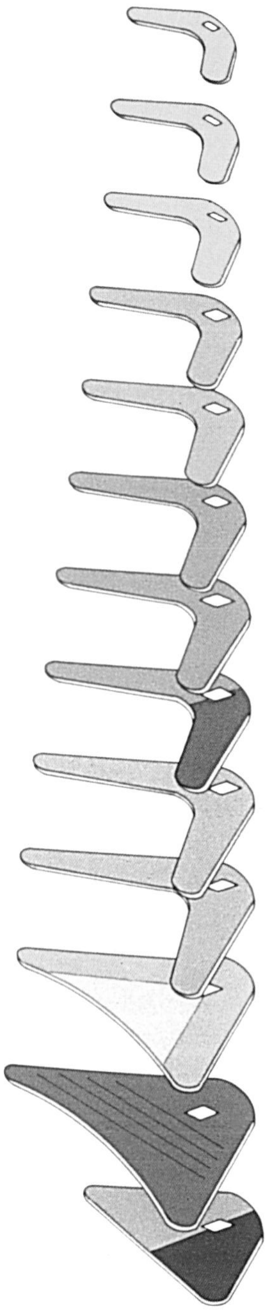

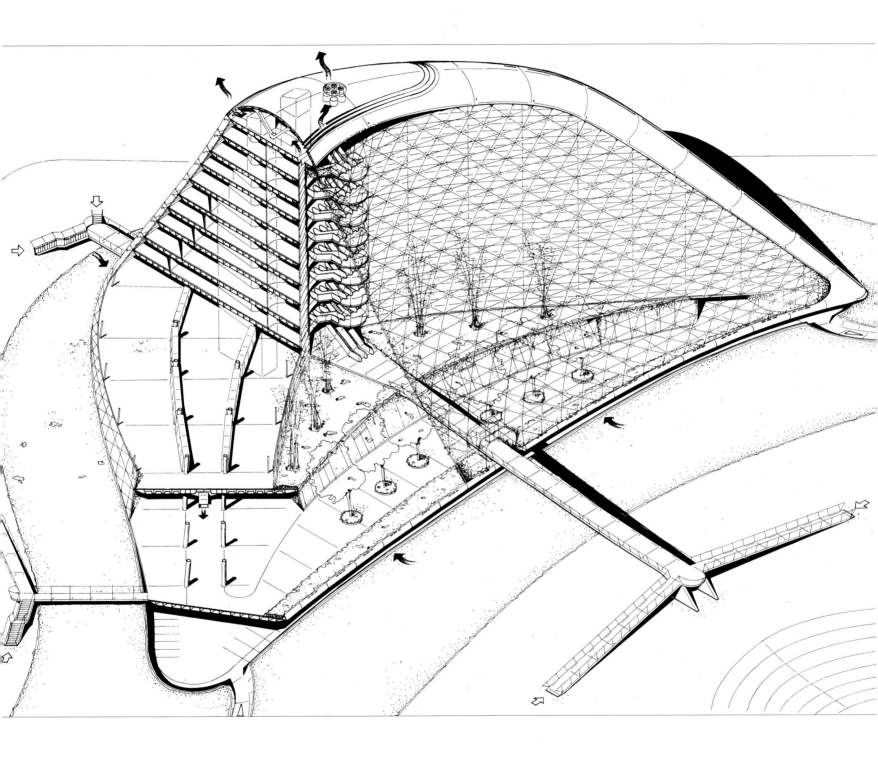

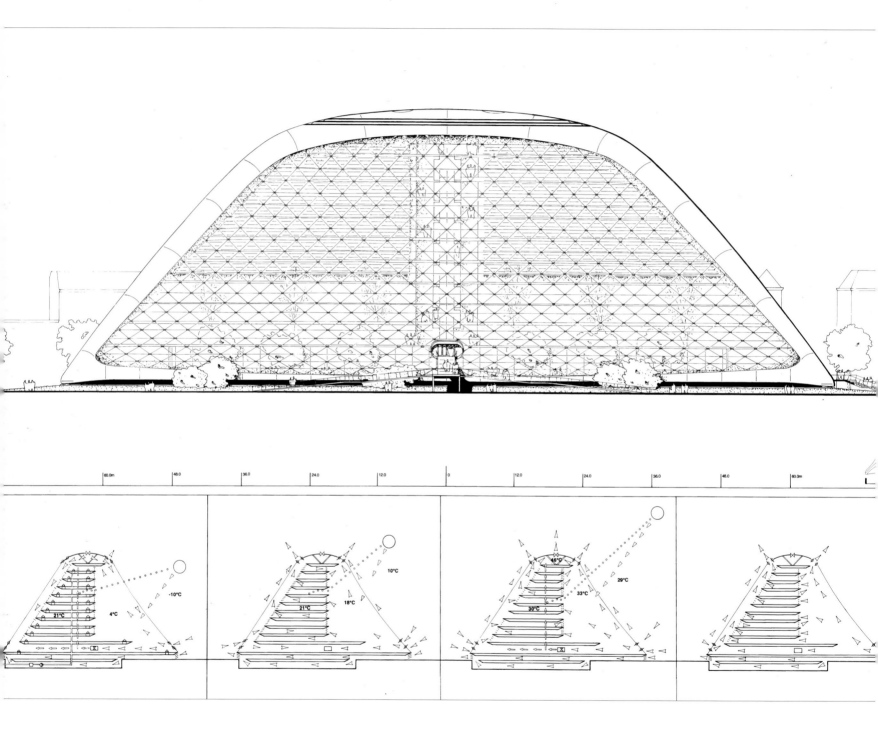

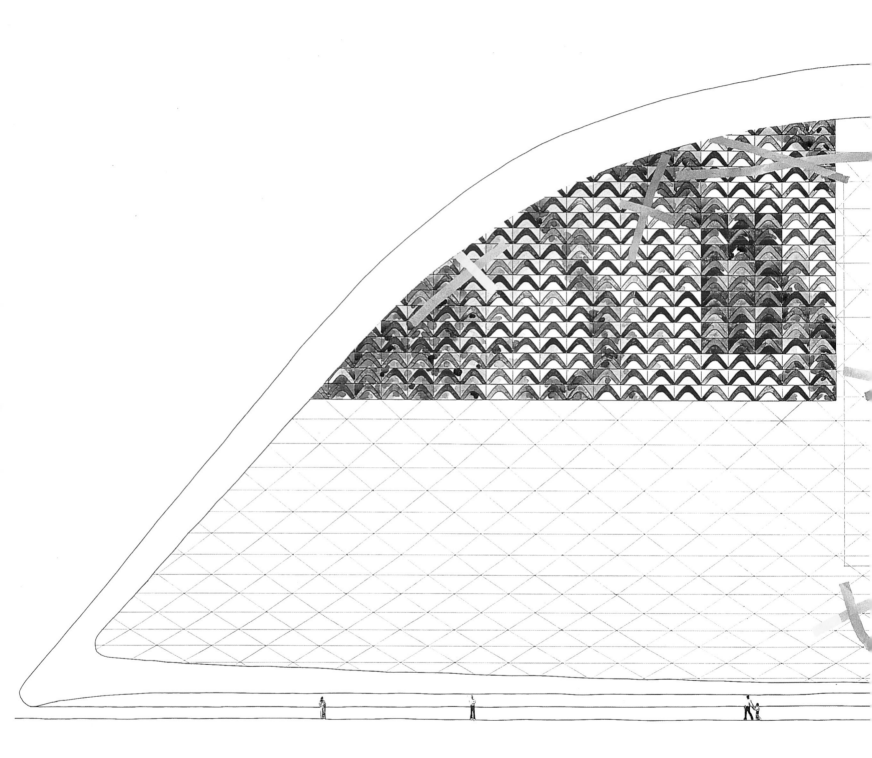

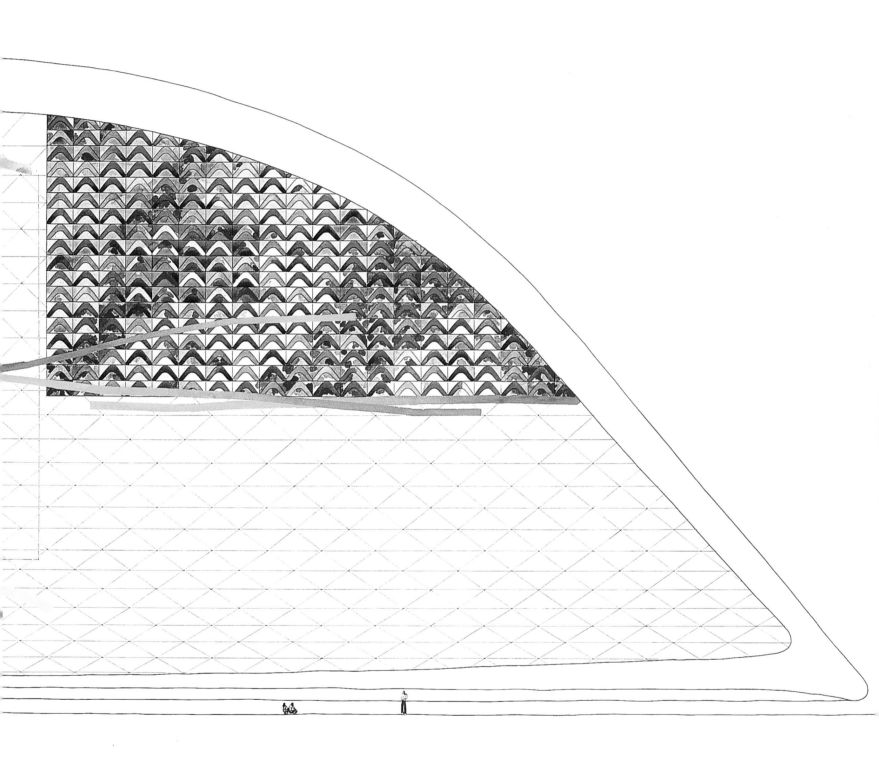

Haus der Energie
Kassel, Germany

This new building, the headquarters of the energy generating company in Kassel, the city famous for its art, was designed by Bieling & Bieling and von Gerkan, Marg & Partners of Hamburg. The whole of the road facing wall of the building is made up of Clarke's glass. Split into two levels, the upper area, a franchised restaurant catering for the daily needs of the 500 employees, is host to a highly coloured and exuberant construction of huge amorphic forms. The central area of each doorway was left clear and transparent by the artist. This achieves numerous ends inducing the retention of substantial ambient white light in the space whilst providing an element of privacy. Also, the relationship between the internal space and the external gardens and major auto-route into the city is harmoniously married. When interviewed about this extraordinary space the office staff from the company expressed great enthusiasm for the 'optimism' it created. Clarke's first proposal of the connected entrance hall, which is a huge and light filled three-storey space was also with substantial colour. Through a series of carefully orchestrated stages he finally settled on a proposal for the removal of the field of colour in favour of white opalescent glass, like milky water. Though transparent, this material acts like a gentle filter of gossamer. The central areas are again left clear, creating the impression of a series of arcades echoing directly the opposite wall of the entrance hall. In this part of the composition Clarke's ability to link internal architectural space with external natural space is at its zenith, and the subtle interplay of colours and transparent tones make this area one of the most remarkable in the recent history of art in architecture.

Architect: *Bieling & Bieling/von Gerkan, Marg & Partners*
Client: *Energie-Aktiengessellschaft Mitteldeutschland*
Project size: *276 sq metres (2971 sq feet)*
Installed: *1993*

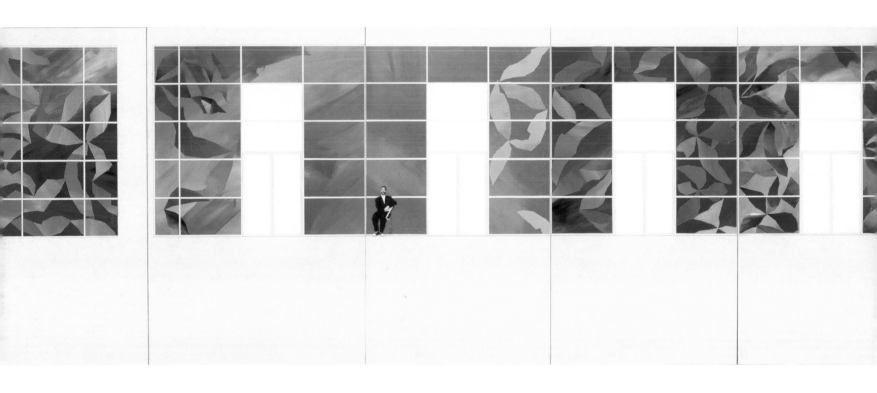

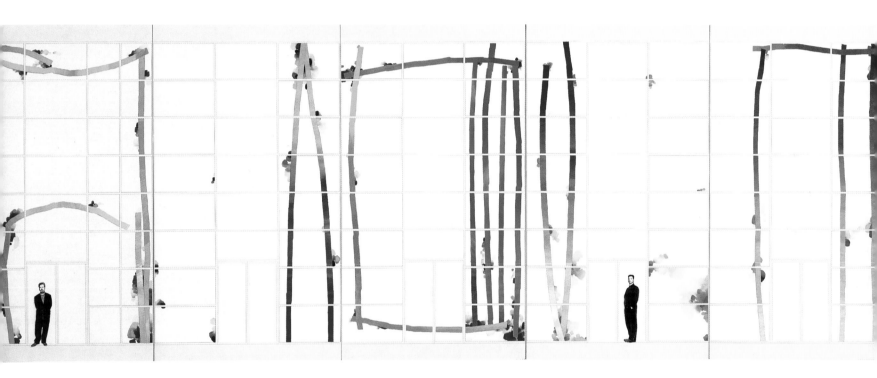

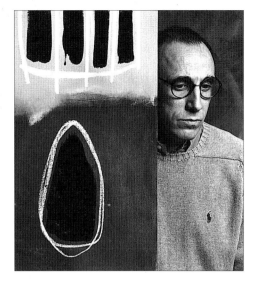

1953: Born Oldham, Lancashire, England.

1965: Began full-time art education at Oldham School of Arts & Crafts (Junior Scholarship).

1968: Burnley School of Art, England.

1970: The North Devon College of Art & Design. First class distinction in Diploma in Art and Design.

1974: Awarded the Winston Churchill Memorial Travelling Fellowship to study art and architecture in Rome, Paris and Germany.

1975: 'Brian Clarke – Glass Art One'. Stained glass, Mid-Pennine Arts Association, Arts Council of Great Britain.
The second part of the Winston Churchill Travelling Fellowship to study contemporary painting in New York and Los Angeles.

1976: Stained glass for the baptistry windows at St Gabriel's Church, Blackburn, England. Architect: FX Verlarde. Stained glass for the east window of All Saints Church, Habergham, England.

1977: Paintings and stained glass for Queen's Medical Centre Chapel, University of Nottingham, England.

1979: 'Brian Clarke Drawings', St Edmunds Art Centre, Salisbury. 'Architectural Stained Glass' edited by Brian Clarke, published by McGraw Hill, New York. 'Glass/Light Exhibition', Festival of The City of London with John Piper and Marc Chagall.
Subject of an Omnibus BBC1 TV documentary, 'Brian Clarke – The Story So Far'.

1980: 'Brian Clarke – Paintings', Mappin Art Gallery & Museum, City of Sheffield, England. Subject of a 'Celebration' Granada TV documentary, 'Brian Clarke'.

1981: Stained glass for the Laver & Barraud's Building, Endell Street, London.
Paintings and stained glass for the lobby of Olympus

Optical Europe GmbH, Headquarters Building, Hamburg, Germany.
'Brian Clarke' by Martin Harrison, published by Quartet Books, London.
'Brian Clarke – New Paintings, Constructions and Prints', The Royal Institute of British Architects, London.

1982: Lived in Düsseldorf, Germany.
Stained glass for the skylight and clerestory, main hall, library and office of the King Khaled International Airport Mosque, Riyadh, Saudi Arabia. Architect: Hellmuth, Obata, Kassabaum.
Lived in Rome, Italy.

1983: 'Brian Clarke – Paintings'. Opening exhibition of the Robert Fraser Gallery, London.

1984: Lived in New York, USA.
Doha Palace. Designed a series of sculptural stained glass and windows for the new Government Building in Doha, Qatar.
Council member of the Winston Churchill Memorial Trust.

1986: Lived in Rome, Italy.
'Brian Clarke – Stained Glass', Seibu Museum of Art, Yurakacho, Tokyo.
Installation of 'Modular Assemblage' for Texas Instruments, Texas, USA.

1987: 'Brian Clarke, Paintings – 1976-1986', Seibu Museum of Art, Tokyo: Yao Seibu Exhibition Hall, Osaka.
'Elan Vital' by Junji Ito, published by the Sezon Museum of Art.
Stained glass for the barrel vaulted roof of the Cavendish Arcade, Derbyshire, England. Architect: Sir Joseph Paxton. Restoration: Derek Latham & Company.
Europa Nostra Award (Prize).
Installation of two Opal Screen windows in Tokyo for the Sezon Museum of Art.

1988: Stained glass for the central lantern tower and skylights of the Lake Sagami Country Club, Yamanishi, Japan. Architect: Arata Isozaki.
Stained glass and Torah shrine for The New Synagogue, Darmstadt, Germany. Architect: Alfred Jacoby.
'Brian Clarke, Malerie und Farbfenster 1977-1988'. The Hessisches Landesmuseum, Darmstadt, Germany.
'Brian Clarke – Intimations of Mortality'. Galerie Karsten Greve, Cologne, Germany.

1989: Fellow of the Royal Society of Arts.
'Brian Clarke – Paintings', The Indar Pasricha Gallery, Hauz Khas, New Delhi, India.
Stained glass for the skylight of the Victoria Quarter, Leeds, England.
Leeds Award for Architecture, 1991 (Prize).
Civic Trust Award, 1991 (Prize).
Arts Council, British Gas, Working for Cities, 1992 (Special Commendation).
Designed the Arena and Stadia stage sets for the Paul McCartney World Tour.

1990: Painting and stained glass for the Cibreo Restaurant, Tokyo. Architect for the interior: Naoki Iijima. Building architect: Nigel Coates.

'Brian Clarke – Into and Out of Architecture', the Mayor Gallery, London.
'Art Random – Brian Clarke' by Paul Beldock, published by Kyoto Shoin.
'Brian Clarke – Architecture and Stained Glass', The Sezon Museum of Art, Tokyo.

1991: Stained glass screen for Glaxo Pharmaceuticals, London. Architect: Skidmore Owings & Merrill.
Stained glass screens and tower for Stansted Airport, Essex, England. Architect: Sir Norman Foster.
Stained glass entrance wall for 100 New Bridge Street, London. Architect: RHWL.
Stained glass skylights for Aram Designs, Heath Street, Hampstead, London.
Stained glass entrance and stairwell windows for 35-38 Chancery Lane, London. In collaboration with sculptor Ivor Abrahams. Architect: BDP.
Entrance wall with onyx, mosaic and stained glass for America House, 1 America Square, London. Architect: RHWL.

1992: Stained glass tower windows for España Telefonica, Placa Catalunya, Barcelona, Spain, for the 1993 Olympiad.
Tapestries and stained glass for The Carmelite, Carmelite Street, London. Architect: Trehearne & Norman.
The Glass Dune – Ministry of the Environment Building, Hamburg, Germany. Architects: Future Systems (Architectural Competition).
Composition incorporating the cladding and colouring to the main facade of the Hôtel du Departement des Bouches-Du-Rhône, Marseille, France. Architect: Alsop & Störmer.

1993: Designed the stadia stage sets for the Paul McCartney 1993 New World Tour.
Stained glass for the north wall of The EAM Building, Kassel, Germany. Architect: Bieling & Bieling.
'The Ruins of Time', stage sets for the ballet by Wayne Eagling in tribute to Rudolph Nureyev. The National Ballet, Amsterdam.
Awarded an Honorary Fellowship to the Royal Institute of British Architects.
Stained glass roofs for The Spindles Shopping Centre, Oldham, England. Architect: Bernard Engle.
'Brian Clarke, Designs on Architecture', Oldham Art Gallery, England.

1994: Made Visiting Professor at The Bartlett Institute of Architecture, University College London.
Stained glass design for Hammersmith Hospital Cancer Centre, London, in association with Future Systems.
Stained glass light-beam design for Crossrail Terminal, Paddington, London. Architect: Alsop and Störmer.
'Brian Clarke – New Paintings', The Karsten Greve Gallery, Milan, Italy.
Designed mosaics and stained glass (and collaborated on interior design with David Chipperfield) for Quartier 206, Friedrichstrasse, Berlin. Architects: Pei, Cobb, Fried and Partners, New York.
Mosaic Floor for Grace Building, Lowe International, New York City.
Designed stained glass and mosaic for Schadow Arkaden, Düsseldorf, Germany. Architect: Walter Brune.